# AMERICAN
★ ★ ★ ★ ★ ★ ★ ★
# CULTURAL
# SHIFTS

Examining the issues that are
tearing our country apart.

AMERICAN

CULTURAL

SHIFTS

# Dr. Alan Scarrow

# AMERICAN CULTURAL SHIFTS

**Examining the Issues That Are Tearing Our Country Apart**
**Dr. Alan Scarrow**

Published and distributed by Merack Publishing.
Library of Congress Control Number: 2022908303
Scarrow, Alan
American Cultural Shifts: Examining the Issues That Are Tearing Our Country Apart
ISBN eBook 978-1-957048-51-2
ISBN Paperback 978-1-957048-52-9
ISBN Hardcover 978-1-957048-53-6

# DEDICATION

To Meera, Evelyn, William and Harrison

# CONTENTS

# CHAPTER 1

★ ★ ★ ★ ★ ★ ★

# WE HATE EACH OTHER

Nations don't last. Throughout antiquity, the most stable, organized tribes and bands of hunter-gatherers left archaeological remains indicating they had survived only two to five centuries. Even the greatest powers the world has ever known—Persia's Achaemenids, Rome, the Tang Dynasty, the Great Mongol Empire, the Dutch and British empires—were unable to maintain their internal cohesiveness and project their strength to the rest of the world for more than several hundred years. Eventually, all of those great world powers collapsed and were consigned to the study of historians following a repetitive historical arc that one day will also claim the greatest empire of the past 100 years —the United States.

*E pluribus unum* is the Latin saying emblazoned on the Great Seal of the United States meaning "out of many, one." It is the miracle that every great power pulls off for some period of time. When a nation is no longer able to remain unified, it declines or divides. What ultimately breaks them is not a lack of food, debt, a weak military, or absence of trade. Rather, the world's great powers break apart for the same reason nations do today, the loss of a common identity that binds people together. Once a society divides, there is little chance of piecing it back together.

That is not to say that history's most powerful societies and nation-states shared similar cultural characteristics. The Great Mongol Empire stretched across all of Asia and Europe, encompassing people of multiple races, religions, and languages. Rome controlled a similar-sized empire but never forced those in its conquered lands to conform to a common language or religion. In fact, throughout history, no society based on racial purity, ethnic cleansing, or religious zealotry has ever become world dominant. What those great empires shared was a belief that they were bound to their neighbors and friends—an unspoken acknowledgment that they were connected and bound to other members of the empire they did not know and never would. The philosopher Ross Poole puts it well. For a nation to exist, its "people don't have to imagine the same nation but they have to imagine that they imagine the same nation."[1]

Alarmingly, the past two decades have given us all kinds of data and abundant examples of behavior that Americans no longer imagine or even imagine that they imagine the same nation. In the past presidential election, 39 percent of Trump supporters and 42 percent of Biden supporters said they had no friends who supported the other candidate.[2] In his inaugural address on January 20, 2021, President Biden described America as being in the middle of an "uncivil war that pits red against

---

1    Ross Poole, *Nation and Identity* (New York, Routledge, 1999), p. 14.

2    Maggie Koerth and Ameilia Thomson-DeVeaux, "Our Radicalized Republic," Fivethirtyeight, January 25, 2021. https://fivethirtyeight.com/features/our-radicalized-republic/#part2.

blue, rural versus urban, conservative versus liberal."[3] Two weeks earlier, Trump supporters had stormed the U.S. Capitol in an attempt to overturn President Trump's defeat in the 2020 election. Four years before that, when President Trump was inaugurated, Trump's opponents burned cars and rioted, leading to 200 arrests made by 8,000 police and the National Guard.[4]

Americans have come to hate each other based on individual political identity. From a sociological perspective, political identity has become the only fair game for hatred. While there remain some who cling to an ugly past of hatred based on race, gender, or sexuality, each successive generation of Americans has become more embracing of differences that are wound into our DNA by chance, not by choice. Even behaviors that at one time were considered the result of individual choices, such as early pregnancy, dropping out of school, or joining a gang, are considered by many liberals to be the result of factors beyond one's control. In their logic, some combination of genetics, family dynamics, community, and social construct compel such behavior, which also occurs by chance, not by choice. But political identity is different. The politics a person chooses to embrace are pure choice, and the act of choosing one's political identity opens the door for others to judge that choice. There are no cable channels dedicated to making a specific race, gender, or sexuality look bad, but there are multiple channels, hundreds of programs, and more websites than one can count to make members of one political

---

3  Perry Bacon Jr., "In America's 'Uncivil War," Republicans Are The Aggressors, February 8, 2021. https://fivethirtyeight.com/features/in-americas-uncivil-war-republicans-are-the-aggressors/.

4  Phil McCausland, Emmanuelle Saliba, Euronews, Erik Ortiz, and Corky Siemaszko, "More Than 200 Arrested in D.D. Protests on Inauguration Day, US. News, January 20, 2017. https://www.nbcnews.com/storyline/inauguration-2017/washington-faces-more-anti-trump-protests-after-day-rage-n709946.

party or the other look foolish, uncaring, stupid, or hypocritical—in short, people worthy of your hate.

Unless you have completely tuned out of politics and social media over the past decade, it is nearly impossible to ignore the hatred directed at conservatives and conservative beliefs. In 2018, Rep. Maxine Waters encouraged her supporters to harass Trump administration officials.[5] Presidential candidate Hillary Clinton described half of Trump supporters belonging to a "basket of deplorables."[6] After a wildfire went through Gatlinburg, Tennessee, leading to fourteen deaths, 200 injuries, and thousands of people being evacuated, one man, presumably a Democrat, posted a tweet that read, "Laughing at all the Trump supporters in Gatlinburg as their homes burn to the ground tonight. Too bad it's not the whole state burning." Another posted, "A few confederate flag flying hillbillies losing their mobile homes isn't newsworthy." Another suggested "Maybe it's 'god' punishing them for voting for Trump."[7]

Biennial national elections are now the litmus test of whether we feel our country belongs to us and whether we belong in it. After the 2016 election, twenty Hollywood stars vowed they were going to leave the

---

5    Jamie Ehrlich, "Maxine Waters encourages supporters to harass Trump administration officials," *CNN* politics, June 25, 2018. https://www.*CNN*.com/2018/06/25/politics/maxine-waters-trump-officials/index.html.

6    Domenico Montanaro, "Hillary Clinton's 'Basket of Deplorables,' in Full Context of This Ugly Campaign," NPR, September 10, 2016. https://tinyurl.com/cx38jne2.

7    "Top of the Ticket," *LA Times*. https://www.latimes.com/opinion/topoftheticket/la-na-tt-americans-hate-20170102-story.html.

country in response to Trump's victory.[8] In 2020, rapper 50 Cent said he would leave the country if Biden was elected.[9] The political whipsaw back and forth from one election to the next over the past two decades is the result of an underlying polarization that defines U.S. politics. Americans have gone from a bell curve distribution of political beliefs and electing politicians within a half-step of center, to a polarized camel hump of firmly held political convictions resulting in the election of Ted Cruz on one end and Bernie Sanders on the other. Party membership has become a tribal identity that quickly distinguishes between "us" and "them." Forty-nine percent of Republicans and 55 percent of Democrats say they are afraid of someone in another political party.[10] Thirty-six percent of Republicans and 27 percent of Democrats see the opposing party as a threat to the nation.[11] This is not just a fear and hatred that hides in the virtual boundaries of social media. In 2010, 33 percent of Democrats and 49 percent of Republicans said they would be somewhat or very disappointed if their child married someone in another political party. Fifty years earlier in 1960, those numbers were 4 percent and 5 percent respectively.[12] Not only do we hate "them" invading our

---

8    Caitlin Greenho, "20 Stars Who Pledged to Leave the Country if Trump Was Elected. Where Are They Now?" Hollywood Reporter, November 10, 2016. https://www.hollywoodreporter.com/lists/20-stars-who-pledged-flee-country-trump-was-elected-are-they-945888.

9    Alex Zidel, "50 Cent Will Leave US If Joe Biden Wins," hnhh Entertainment, October 21, 2020. https://www.hotnewhiphop.com/50-cent-will-leave-us-if-joe-biden-wins-news.119985.html.

10    Steven Levitsky and Daniel Ziblatt, *How Democracies Die* (New York: Crown, 2018) p.167.

11    "Political Polarization in the American Public," Pew Research, June 12, 2014. https://www.pewresearch.org/politics/2014/06/12/political-polarization-in-the-american-public/.

12    Levitsky and Ziblatt, *How Democracies Die*, 167.

*Facebook* feeds and chat rooms, we darn sure don't want them ruining family discussions at the dinner table.

In a recent study that awarded a hypothetical scholarship to a student based on GPA, race, and political party affiliation, the most polarizing variable was the student's political party. Study participants were more split on awarding scholarship money based on the political identity of the hypothetical student than GPA or race,[13] presumably because political identity was a better reflection of the candidate's character and capacity for making good choices.

Americans have entered a state of negative polarization. It's not so much that we like our own party, we just hate the other because we fear our opponent wants to rule and dominate us. In effect, negative polarization is the first symptom of demonization. Between 2000 and 2012, people who liked their own party more than they disliked the opposition went from 61 percent to 38 percent, while the number who disliked the opposition more than they liked their own party went from 20 percent to 42 percent.[14] This political extremist environment that hums in the background while we try to engage the opposition has all but ruined political discourse.

Political extremism by itself is not necessarily bad for a nation. On the contrary, extremist ideas have served our country well. The abolition of slavery, women's suffrage, and civil rights were, at one moment in our history, extremist ideas. Thankfully, with time, endless amounts of work, heroic sacrifice, and too much violence, ideas that were once extreme became mainstream tenets of our culture. But when both political parties flock to the extremes with no common ground in the middle,

---

13    Ezra Klein, *Why We're Polarized* (New York, Avid Reader Press, 2020), p. 75.

14    "Feelings about partisans and the parties," Pew Research. https://www. pewresearch.org/politics/2016/06/22/1-feelings-about-partisans-and-the-parties/.

progress stops, hatred flourishes, and the loss of a common national identity begins.

Political extremism and the demonization that follows in its wake come to a head every four years during presidential elections. Presidential election campaigns have shifted from trying to influence independent voters to motivating the base. The reason is simple. There are very few true independents to influence. Surveys report 38 percent of Americans claim they are independent, but when it comes to the presidential race, most voters who identify as independent have already made up their mind. A more accurate number of truly independent voters is likely around 7 percent.[15]

Congressional races have been similar in their focus on motivating the base and mirror Presidential races. Today, more than 90 percent of House elections and the vast majority of Senate elections are won by the candidate who is in the same party as the president who carries that district or state.[16] Party loyalty and straight ticket voting has increased so dramatically that even the election of local officials mimics the Presidential election outcome. As a result, personalities and voting records matter much less than in the past. The more a congressional candidate walks and talks like the favored Presidential candidate in that geographic area, the better the chances of getting elected. Blount County, Alabama, the most politically conservative county in America, is every bit as likely to elect a Republican candidate[17] as Berkshire

---

15    Klein, *Why We're Polarized,* 71.

16    Alan I. Abramowitz, *The Great Alignment* (New Haven, Connecticut: Yale University Press, 2018), p. 95.

17    "The Most Republican County in Each State," HUFFPOST. https://tinyurl.com/8kmnzy8.

County, Massachusetts, the most liberal county in America, is to elect a Democratic candidate.[18]

If a congressional incumbent is going to be ousted, the challenger is best served by being more of whatever the incumbent is perceived to be. Challengers to incumbents in Republican congressional races mostly come from the political right of the incumbent, while challengers to incumbents in Democratic congressional races come from the political left of the incumbent.[19] Moderate candidates that used to have an electability advantage over ideological extremists have almost evaporated.

The same polarization holds true of state legislature elections. A generation ago, it was not uncommon for political control in state legislatures to flip back and forth between the parties with more frequency than the Olympic Games. Between 1990 and 2010, control between Republicans and Democrats in the Indiana House of Representatives flipped six times.[20] A more moderate national voter base created an environment that was politically flexible and constantly ripe for change.

That is no longer the case. In the second decade of the twenty-first century, red and blue are in, violet is out. Today, only one state (Minnesota) has a legislature that is divided between the two parties. Of the remaining forty-nine, thirty-one are controlled by Republicans and eighteen by Democrats. Thirty-seven states have both houses of the legislature and the governor in the same party, twenty-four Republican and thirteen

---

18    Thomas C. Frohlich and Alexander Kent, "The Most Democratic County in Every State," October 8, 2016. https://247wallst.com/special-report/2016/10/08/the-most-democratic-county-in-every-state/6/.

19    Klein, *Why We're Polarized*, 179.

20    Alan Greenblatt, "All or Nothing: How State Politics Became a Winner-Take-All World, December 17, 2018. https://www.governing.com/archive/gov-state-politics-governors-2019.html.

Democrat, with Democrats dominating the West and Northeast and Republicans dominating in the Southeast and Midwest.[21]

Polarization is not just a phenomenon of the past two decades. We have been sorting ourselves into like-minded communities for a long time. In 1976, less than 25 percent of Americans lived in a county where the presidential election was a landslide. By 2004, half of all voters lived in landslide counties, and in 2020, it was 58.2 percent.[22] The result is Balkanized communities whose inhabitants find those not in their political camp to be culturally incomprehensible. Americans are now the least likely out of citizens from twelve countries to talk about politics with people holding different worldviews.[23] We prefer the company we keep to be as politically similar to us as possible.

We achieve similar company by sorting ourselves into political groups based largely on where we choose to live—amidst the urban buzz and suburban sprawl of cities or the relative quiet and solitude of rural towns and the countryside. Today there is a marked distinction between the political ideologies of rural and urban Americans. The world may be getting flatter, but ironically, where you choose to live matters more than ever. The chance of you living in a community where almost everyone thinks like you went from one in twenty in 1992, to one in five today.[24] Currently, few metro areas vote Republican and few rural areas

---

21    David French, *Divided We Fall: America's Secession Threat and How to Restore Our Nation* (New York, *St. Martin's Press, 2020),* p. 31.

22    Bill Bishop, "For Most Americans, the Local Presidential Vote Was a Landslide," The Daily Yonder, December 17, 2020. https://dailyyonder.com/for-most-americans-the-local-presidential-vote-was-a-landslide/2020/12/17/.

23    Diane Mutz, *Hearing the Other Side: Deliberative versus Participatory Democracy* (Cambridge: Cambridge University Press, 2020). doi:10.1017/CBO9780511617201.

24    Klein, *Why We're Polarized,* 38.

vote Democrat, with the cutoff line at around 900 people per square mile. The denser the population, the more concentrated the Democratic affiliation.[25] Sixty-five percent of Republicans say they want to live in communities where houses are larger and further apart, with schools and shopping a distance away, while 61 percent of Democrats want to live in areas with smaller homes that are closer together with shopping and schools within walking distance.[26]

Once we get into our preferred living zone, we become fixed in our political space. From 1972 to 1984, the average difference between how a state voted in one presidential election compared to the next was 7.7 percent. From 2000 to 2012, it dropped to 1.9 percent.[27] Not only do we prefer the company we keep to be similar to us, we also intend to stay in the geographic company of similarly minded people over time.

Rural voters and voters from communities under 50,000 make up only 30 percent of the U.S. voting population.[28] In the past, barriers of distance and organization kept rural voters from acting together politically. Social media has reduced those barriers, making it just as easy for rural voters to identify and share stories of their political frustrations as urban dwellers. Those frustrations have grown significantly for rural Americans. Since 1980, rural communities have been hurt by two processes that have been a boon to urban communities—an explosion of knowledge and globalization. An explosion of knowledge, driven by the ever-increasing ease of sharing ideas, has encouraged specialization and thus a rapid increase in the size of cities where the collective body

---

25    Klein, *Why We're Polarized*, 39.

26    Klein, *Why We're Polarized*, 42.

27    Klein, *Why We're Polarized*, 38.

28    Peter Zeihan, *Disunited Nations: The Scramble for Power in an Ungoverned World* (New York: HarperCollins, 2020), loc. 4893, Kindle.

of knowledge, skills, and resources is greater. Globalization has further driven cities to specialization, as worldwide demand rewards companies and organizations that can scale their products and services. Examples include San Francisco and Seattle in internet technology, Boston and Memphis in biomedical services, Houston in oil and natural gas extraction, and New York in financial services. In each of those examples, a nidus of specialized companies has drawn in more people with important knowledge and skills. As the core group of talent and resources grows, it acts as a gravitational pull, adding even more depth to the labor force of the particular city. In contrast, rural communities simply don't have the people and resources to compete with urban areas. This has driven a nationalist agenda of "America First" deep into rural areas that resonates with people who feel left out.

Since globalization affects rural areas beyond the U.S. borders, it is no surprise that the same rural versus urban political distinction has been occurring around the world. In the United Kingdom, rural voters were Brexit supporters while Londoners overwhelmingly voted to remain in the European Union, which gave them better opportunities for trade. In France, support for Marine Le Pen and her nationalist views come from rural voters, while Parisians support Emmanuel Macron and the more liberal En Marche! party. In Germany, support for the anti-European Union and nationalist party Alternative for Germany (AfD) came from rural voters, while urban Frankfurters favored the Christian Democratic Union/Christian Social Union of Chancellor Angela Merkel.

An explosion of knowledge and the reach of globalization are largely economic issues. Economics may say a lot about a community's business climate, productivity, and unemployment, but it doesn't reflect the moral and religious foundation of the community. From a moral and religious perspective, rural and urban dwellers are choosing very different paths, with rural Americans favoring a religious leaning Republican party and urban Americans siding with the less religious Democratic party.[29] In 2002, 50 percent of Republicans and 52 percent of Democrats said it wasn't necessary to believe in God to be a moral person. Fifteen years later in 2017, 47 percent of Republicans and 64 percent of Democrats felt the same way.[30] Strong feelings about morality and religion correlate with church attendance, and the map of church attendance in the United States is essentially the same as the map of partisan voting habits. Lowest church attendance states vote predominantly Democrat, and the highest vote Republican.[31] A moral and religious divide amongst people that already have differences over political ideology only drives the hatred toward one another deeper.

The map of partisan voting and church attendance is also similar to the map of gun ownership. Just like fluid sexual identity has become a central and successful issue for the left, gun rights advocates have had similar success on the right preaching to a rural, Republican base that treats gun ownership rights with the same depth of respect given to wedding vows. In 1986, thirty-one states had "no carry" laws, which prevented citizens from carrying firearms. Remarkably, twenty-nine states now have "shall carry" laws that allow people to carry firearms if they can lawfully own one. Eight states have a "constitutional carry," which essentially uses the 2nd Amendment as the only necessary permission to carry a firearm. Zero states continue to have a "no carry" law.[32] Constitutional carry is to Democrats what multiple genders are to Republicans, a hard stop issue that brings out the worst in everyone and stokes the fires of fear and hate even hotter.

---

29    "Party affiliation," Pew Research. https://www.pewforum.org/religious-landscape-study/party-affiliation/.

30    Klein, *Why We're Polarized*, 38.

31    French, *Divided We Fall*, 32.

32    French, *Divided We Fall*, 88.

With an abundance of fear and hate between political parties, there is surprisingly little comfort found within the parties. In the Republican Party, 75 percent of members identify as conservative, but within the six subgroups of the party—business, national security advocates, fiscal conservatives, evangelicals, pro-lifers, and populists—infighting is common over whose agenda should take center stage. Each subgroup cares deeply about its own core issue but has little concern for the issues of their fellow Republicans. That single focus makes Republicans favor candidates who are uncompromising and rigid in defense of their specific agenda.

In comparison, only half of Democrats identify themselves as liberals, and the Democratic tent has become so big that the party looks like a collection of interest groups. Single mothers disagree with the youth vote on subsidizing college tuition. Environmentalists and unions spar over industrial policy. Gays and African Americans define equal rights very differently. Most African Americans, Hispanics, and union members are economically liberal but socially conservative. Conversely, most gays and single women tend to be economically conservative but socially liberal. The big tent compels Democrats to favor those willing to compromise, and results in putting candidates up for election whom party members tolerate but rarely inspire. Thus, neither party offers much refuge for people who, at least superficially, share much of the same political ideology.

The hate between people of differing political ideologies doesn't just evaporate into the ether after a Presidential election. There are consequences when our emotional vessels are filled with fear and hate. History shows us how this can play out. There have been times when fear and hatred overflowed America's emotional vessel. In 1860, the southern states believed their culture and fundamental liberties were under attack. At that time, Southerners shared a common faith and a distinct way of life and became irrationally fearful that Northerners wanted to harm them. The next four years of the Civil War and the ensuing period of Reconstruction nearly broke our country apart. But it didn't. We fought, healed a bit, and eventually the next several generations of Americans carried on believing that our common strengths were more important than our unique differences.

America's great run will end one day. What we must decide is whether this generation will be the one to see it end or if our story will continue. That is the purpose of this book and what we will explore and analyze over the remaining thirteen chapters.

# CHAPTER 2

★ ★ ★ ★ ★ ★ ★

# HATE SERVES A POLITICAL END

Seneca, one of the great Roman Stoics, left behind insights that have influenced philosophers and academics throughout the ages. One of his most controversial observations concerned politicians and religion, "Religion is regarded by the common people as true, by the wise as false, and by rulers as useful." Seneca was pointing out the subtle interplay between deeply held beliefs, human emotion, and politics. His artful way of playing with words was, as Picasso might say, the lie that shows us the truth.[33]

The notion that leaders and politicians manipulate the beliefs and emotions of their constituents is hardly a revelation. As long as there

---

33    1946 Copyright, Picasso: Fifty Years of His Art by Alfred H. Barr Jr., Chapter: Statement by Picasso: 1923, Quote Page 270, Column 1, The Museum of Modern Art, New York.

have been politicians, there has been manipulation. The best politicians learn how to manipulate their audience's emotions without appearing to do so. The right words by the right leader at the right time have resulted in political movements that changed the world. Occasionally, those words are upbeat and inspiring. The calm, non-rhotic rhythm of a John F. Kennedy speech, the folksy optimism of Ronald Reagan, the carefully chosen words of Winston Churchill, or the beautiful arcing pitch of Martin Luther King are rare examples of leaders that could deliver an inspirational message while weathering attacks from their adversaries. More commonly, the words used by politicians to stir their audience are ones of fear and hate.

Hate is a much stronger political motivator than love. People feel satisfied when they have something to vote for but are exhilarated when there is something to vote against. Voters may tell surveyors that they are turned off by negative campaigning, but the truth is that they are riveted and entertained by negative politics. They say they hate negative political ads, but they can easily recall exactly what's in them. Winning politicians know what voters want, but the most effective ones intimately know what voters hate. The Russian playwright Anton Chekhov understood this human characteristic when he wrote, "Love, friendship and respect do not unite people as much as a common hatred for something.[34]

Hate does not just appear out of thin air among voters. It is preceded and accompanied by fear. Hate may be the most proximate emotion regarding a political adversary, but first the adversary must be enough of a threat to draw attention. George Lucas cleverly outlined the relationship between fear and hate. He gave Yoda one of the best lines in the entire Star Wars saga. "Fear leads to anger, anger leads to hate,

---

34    Anton Chekhov, quote, LIBQUOTES. https://libquotes.com/anton-chekhov/quote/lbi8b0a.

hate leads to suffering."[35] We pay attention to our fears. Fear triggers the most primal portions of our brain to command our bodies to find an escape or to turn and fight. Fear of loss is a motivator two-and-a-half times more powerful than the desire for gain.[36]

Our fears become magnified by social media and a 24/7 news cycle because we are more connected than ever to our political adversaries. A constant stream of stories intended to promote outrage comes at us each day. The issue within the story is not as important as who is involved and, more importantly, how those within our political tribe are responding. The fear and hate triggered by our adversary can only be offset by the feeling of safety when our thoughts are in sync with those in our own political tribe.

Tribes form around political movements. The Tea Party, Black Lives Matter, #MeToo, Brexit, Occupy Wall Street, the Green New Deal, and the March for Our Lives all spawned millions of supporters. And enemies. Big tech, big government, rich people, gun manufacturers, liberals, nationalists, cops, and powerful white men all became targets of hate by one or more of those political movements. "Mass movements can rise and spread without a belief in God, but never without a belief in a devil,"[37] said philosopher Eric Hoffer. Leaders of those movements understood how to use that sentiment to their advantage.

People crave certainty and resounding truths. They like being part of movements equipped with those truths and certainties, and if there are

---

35    Yoda, quote, PLANET YODA. https://tinyurl.com/4yzpk4hz.

36    Brian Tracy, *How the Best Leaders Lead* (New York: AMACOM, 2010), loc. 2249, Kindle.

37    "Summary of Eric Hoffer's, 'The True Believer,' Reasoning and Meaning," September 4, 2017. https://reasonandmeaning.com/2017/09/04/summary-of-eric-hoffers-the-true-believer/.

rebels or heretics involved, all the better. Political movements of the past decade nailed those desires. Followers of the Tea Party were just as convinced of the righteousness of their cause and the evilness of their enemies as the followers of Black Lives Matter. But one man's freedom fighter is another man's terrorist. No matter how righteous the cause looks from the inside, from the outside, if they are not "us," they are "them" and worthy of hate.

When violence becomes part of a political movement, hate deepens. Demonstrators protesting the police killing of George Floyd in the summer of 2020 became part of a growing political movement against police brutality and racially motivated violence. Perhaps there was a window of time when those outside of that political movement were supportive of it. But video of demonstrators tearing down the front façades of homes and businesses in Portland, Seattle, Minneapolis, and Louisville while asking for police departments to be defunded only amplified the hate people outside their political tribe had for them. The same thing happened on January 6, 2021, when Trump supporters broke into the U.S. Capitol, tore through offices, and behaved like thugs. Their insistence that the presidential election was stolen and the violence that ensued was an affirmation to people outside their political tribe that Trump supporters were people worthy of hate.

There is a tendency to judge members of a group by their least worthy member. Although manifestly unfair, there is some justification. The character and destiny of a group are often determined by its most distasteful actions. Still, it is frustrating to be grouped together with people who may share our political ideology but whose behavior we find inexplicable. We feel compelled to account for behavior that we don't condone. This is not a new frustration. The game of history is usually played by the best and worst over the heads of the majority in the middle. Possessing a political ideology closer to the middle is like playing tennis at the net while two big gun players bellow at each other on the baselines with each stroke of their racket.

At one baseline is a party that is pragmatic but heartless and on the other a party that is compassionate but imprudent. Conservative Republicans see the world as a constant battle between good and evil. They glorify those that they believe live by solid, traditional values and demonize those they see as a threat to undermine those values. Liberal Democrats see the world as a battle between the powerful and the powerless. In their eagerness, liberals see the powerless as objects and not independent actors capable of creating or undermining their own power. The late senator Daniel Patrick Moynihan describes it eloquently, "The central conservative truth is that it is culture, not politics, that determines the success of a society. The central liberal truth is that politics can change a culture and save it from itself."[38]

Republicans and Democrats use each other like a knife and whetstone. The words and behavior of one party hone the message of outrage and hate of the other. Through that process, politicians become adept at using their political enemies to their advantage. Enemies help give a political movement coherence. They provide someone to blame and thus some ability to know what to expect. Enemies are real, quantifiable, and often predictable. They make the world seem less disorganized and paradoxically less dangerous. Enemies create the illusion that things can be won, situations overturned, and trends renounced. They counteract apathy. Enemies fuel the underlying psychology of politics that make emotional manipulation feel natural.

---

38   Jonah Goldberg, "Something is wrong when lifeguards are fired for saving lives," *National Review* website, July 6, 2012. https://www.nationalreview.com/2012/07/politics-and-symptoms-sick-culture-jonah-goldberg/.

For example, few people have trouble believing that the Jet Propulsion Lab can land rovers on Mars and send back video of the red planet. We don't doubt that antibiotics can cure pneumonia, or that nuclear bombs are real, or that drunk drivers are dangerous. But how about climate change? If one were to strike up a conversation about climate change at a local or neighborhood coffee shop anywhere near where I live in southwest Missouri, there would almost certainly be a robust debate about whether climate change is even real. It's not as if there isn't ample objective evidence for each of those examples. The JPS rovers have sent back hours of video from their travels across Mars. Millions of people around the world have been prescribed antibiotics and cured of pneumonia. Nuclear bombs have been detonated, and drunk drivers kill thousands of people every year. Similarly, there is objective evidence for climate change. Sea levels have been rising by one-third of a meter per century, the North Pole ice cap is breaking apart, atmospheric carbon dioxide levels are higher than at any time in the last four million years, and twenty of the hottest years on record have occurred since 2000.[39] Yet none of that data is persuasive to those who doubt climate change is real.

The reason climate change is different from Mars rovers, antibiotics, nuclear bombs, or drunk drivers is that climate change has become a political topic. When data betrays our political instinct, we abandon the data for the answer we want, and what we want is an answer that is consistent with what we already believe. Among people who are skeptical of climate change, the more they learn about climate change, the more skeptical they become. There's a difference between searching for the best evidence and searching for the best evidence that proves us right. "Faced with the choice of changing one's mind and proving there is no need to do so, almost everyone gets busy on the proof," said

---

39    Marcia Bjornerud, *Timefulness, How Thinking Like a Geologist Can Save the World* (Princeton, NJ: Princeton University Press, 2018), pp. 127–128.

economist John Kenneth Galbraith. He was so on point. Our political fights today are more about who we think we are rather than over differences of opinion. People don't pick their party affiliation based on a self-generated opinion of a particular policy, rather they adjust their opinion based on their political party affiliation.

Today each party has taken a side with regard to race, religion, and ideological and cultural issues. Those sides were not so obvious decades ago because there was so much overlap between the parties. Democrats of the 1990s were tough on crime and illegal immigration,[40] while Republicans stumped for universal free trade and a global economy.[41] The same type of party partisanship affects politicians directly. Having declared their loyalty to one party or the other, legislators think less about how this affects their constituency and more about what their party's position on the issue is.

Psychologist Jonathan Haidt has a persuasive way of describing our thinking in this regard, "Our moral thinking is much more like a politician looking for votes than a scientist looking for the truth."[42] The research on reasoning demonstrates that it has evolved not to help us find the truth but rather to help engage in arguments, persuasion, and manipulation during discussions with others. Skilled arguers are not after truth but rather arguments in support of their views.

Each of us has a little politician inside our brains looking and hoping for information that confirms our beliefs. In a sense, we are all compelled

---

40    Philip Bump, "Breaking: The Democratic Party is different now than it was in 1995," *The Washington Post*, June 6, 2017. https://tinyurl.com/2dwj6nkj.

41    Michael Lind, "Six New Policies for America in the 90s," *Christian Science Monitor*, September 8, 1995. https://www.csmonitor.com/1995/0908/08181.html.

42    Jonathan Haidt, *The Righteous Mind: Why Good People Are Divided by Politics and Religion* (New York, Pantheon, 2012), p. 89.

to think like politicians whether we want to admit it or not. Those with little engagement in politics look at a policy and wonder how it will affect them, while those that are very engaged in politics wonder what supporting a policy says about them. It is one of the reasons behind the saying in conservative circles that politics is "downstream from culture," a saying that was part of the inspiration for this book.

Sadly, thinking like a politician is often unfulfilling. Of all the ways to find meaning in life, politics is one of the unhappiest because the ambitions it strives for almost always go unachieved. Finding purpose in politics means lacing it with passion and often a rage that perverts the whole process. When people disagree and argue about the best amenable outcome, that is negotiation. But when one finds their whole purpose in life is to reside in disagreement, the chances of ever finding an amicable solution fade quickly. That is the situation we find ourselves in today.

We weren't always this way. It has taken years for our hatred toward our political opponents to evolve to a fever pitch. The next few chapters will look at the factors that have driven that hate.

★ ★ ★ ★ ★ ★ ★

# CHAPTER 3

# INEQUALITY: INCOME, WEALTH, POWER, AND TRUST

Once a month, I travel through southwest Missouri and northwest Arkansas to take calls at one of the hospitals my neurosurgery group covers. It's a trip that takes me past several small rural towns that unfortunately have seen better days. A typical downtown area that once had stores for groceries, clothes, mechanics, and hardware has largely been shuttered. In its place are evangelical churches, government offices, sometimes a bar. Mostly there are empty buildings. The outskirts of town are home to the only meaningful commerce, usually in the form of a Walmart or Dollar General store and a gas station. Since I am frequently called to the emergency rooms of hospitals in this area, I see the results of the drug problems that plague these towns. I am reminded of those patients as I drive through. On the whole, it's not an uplifting picture. Signs of hope are rare.

I empathize with the people living in these communities. The closed stores and empty buildings remind me of where I grew up—a town that has been hit by similar economic realities and hardships. The patients I see here often make me think of the people I grew up with. Their combination of pride, humility, a touch of shyness, and a palpable attachment to their community and the land feels familiar. I also know that if my truck were to break down anywhere near one of these towns, that very capable help would happily appear within minutes. It may not be an uplifting drive, but it is one where I always feel safe.

When I talk to patients from these towns, I sometimes sense a notable loss of dignity. The stability of good paying manufacturing jobs is mostly gone, replaced by an insecurity that accompanies service and retail jobs that are a good side hustle but don't offer the wages and benefits to sustain a family. The community's churches that once bound its members together with common beliefs and values are now cast as irrational and backwards by people who claim to know better. Towns once large enough to provide for a local high school—a source for education on weekdays and community pride on Friday nights—are no longer capable of doing so.

It was not always this way. A great divide has opened up between the haves and have-nots in our country. Whether the divide is defined in terms of income, wealth, education, or power, the ruling class and working class are headed in opposite directions.

From 1946 to 1980, income in the United States increased fairly consistently across all categories of income from lowest to highest. Then a transition occurred. From 1980 to 2014, incomes for the top 1 percent of wage earners increased dramatically, while the lowest 20 percent of income earners saw their wages decrease.[43] In that same period after 1980, the top 10 percent of wage earners took home 48 percent of all wages,[44] while the share of total wages for the top 1 percent of wage earners went from 11 percent to 20 percent.[45] This shift of more income going to those who were already taking home higher wages is the result of three forces: technology, globalization, and the concentration of power.

As technology gets woven into nearly every job, a premium is paid to those that can use technology to increase their productivity. For workers, more education provides them with opportunities to use new technology, making them more valuable to their employers. For example, a business analyst who learns to use artificial intelligence (AI) to perform sales and business forecasting has a distinct advantage over a business analyst who doesn't have those skills. In general, the more education, the greater the wage. As such, over the past several decades, wages for college graduates have increased more than for high school graduates, and wages for those with post-graduate degrees have increased even more.[46] Globalization only compounds the wage benefits of those with more education as a larger market creates greater demand for both the skills they possess and the products they produce.

A concentration of power also results in higher wages but does so in a way that is more divisive and engenders hate. In 1978, the average CEO made thirty times the average worker's salary. In 2016, it was 271 times the average worker's salary. Over that period of time, CEO pay has gone up 950 percent compared to 11 percent for the average worker

---

43    Daniel Susskind, *World Without Work* (New York, Henry Holt, 2020), p. 136.

44    Binyamin Applebaum, *The Economists' Hour: False Prophets, Free Markets, and the Fracture of Society* (New York: Hachette, 2019), p. 326.

45    Susskind, *World Without Work*, 137.

46    Susskind, *World Without Work,* 102.

and 70 percent faster than the stock market.[47] The highest paid CEOs make well over $100 million in salary annually. Elon Musk, CEO of Tesla, made nearly $600 million in 2020.[48] Doug McMillon, CEO of Walmart, made over 1000 times the median salary of a Walmart employee in 2017.[49] In New York, the ratio of income for the top 1 percent compared to the other 99 percent is 45 to 1, and for many executives, the ratio of salary compared to their average worker is 300 to 1. This is hard to find at any other point in history. In Rome AD 14, the average Roman senator had a salary one hundred times that of the average worker, and legion commanders received a salary forty-five times the average worker.[50]

It is not a sin to make a lot of money. In fact, it is the unapologetic dream of many Americans to do so. But income from salaries is different from income generated by labor or commissions. Those who make exorbitant money from salary alone are perceived to have not taken risks or avoided investing in the sweat equity of a growing business.

Individuals who have gotten large sums of money by inheritance suffer a similar perception. The list of people who have become exceedingly wealthy from family inheritance is growing rapidly. In the last fifteen years, the number of billionaires in the United States who have inherited their wealth has increased by 50 percent.[51] Both high salaried individuals

---

47    Simon Sinek, *The Infinite Game* (Penguin Random House, 2019), p. 75.

48    "Word's top 5 highest paid CEOs of 2020," The Business Standard website, December 7, 2020. https://www.tbsnews.net/world/worlds-top-5-highest-paid-ceos-2020-142288.

49    Ben Wittstein, "Highest paid CEOs in America," Stacker, January 26, 2021. https://stacker.com/stories/1255/highest-paid-ceos-america.

50    Michael O'Sullivan, *The Levelling: What's Next After Globalization* (New York: Hachette, 2019), p. 40.

51    Susskind, *World Without Work*, 177.

and those with inherited fortunes are people who have found a loophole that makes their income appear a little too easy. In the growing divide between the haves and have-nots, those with too much easy money are easy to hate.

The financial divide between the haves and have-nots is even more pronounced when analyzing differences in wealth. Wealth, in comparison to income, is the capital or assets owned by an individual. Inequality measured by wealth in the United States is almost double that of inequality measured by income.[52] The wealthiest 1 percent owns 40 percent of all wealth, while the wealthiest 10 percent own 70 percent of all wealth,[53] and the richest 0.1 percent of Americans—around 160,000 people—own 22 percent of all wealth. Shockingly, those 160,000 people have as much wealth as the poorest 90 percent combined.[54]

Wealth tends to accumulate over time within the ownership class. When the return on wealth rises faster than the economy as a whole, those who own the capital become even wealthier in comparison to their workers. Furthermore, as technology drives greater productivity, and in many cases replaces human labor, there is less need for workers. Less need for workers results in lower wages for those workers. For example, robots that weld faster and more precisely than human welders make a metal fabricating company more productive. Robots also decrease that company's need for human welders. The added productivity means more profit for the owners and shareholders of the company but less demand for human welders and thus lower wages for the workers.

---

52    Jonathan Haskel and Stian Westlake, *Capitalism Without Capital* (Princeton, NJ: Princeton University Press, 2018), p. 120.

53    O'Sullivan, *The Levelling*, 41.

54    Susskind, *World Without Work*, 145.

As a result of technology, globalization, and a concentration of power, a fault line has developed in economic growth. Corporate profits relative to gross domestic product (GDP) are at an all-time high, benefitting owners and shareholders, while wages relative to GDP are at an all-time low, hurting workers. Similarly, the average wage relative to the overall stock market value is at a multi-decade low,[55] and while almost half of all households own shares of stock, the richest 10 percent of households control 84 percent of the total stock market value.[56] So while a rising economic tide lifts all boats, if you don't own a boat, you may just drown.

The picture that begins to emerge from this income and wealth data is that we are a country that is polarized economically, which mirrors the way we are polarized politically. An ownership class (the haves) has distinguished itself from the working class (the have-nots). From that perspective, the rise in support for socialism, infusing $5.5 trillion of government money into the economy in response to the Covid-19 pandemic,[57] and greater redistribution of wealth, particularly amongst the millennial generation (those born between 1981 and 1996), makes more sense. In 1989 when the average baby boomer was thirty-five, their generation owned 21 percent of all wealth. In 2008 when the average Gen Xer was 35, their generation owned 8 percent of all wealth. The average millennial turns 35 in 2023. Today their generation owns only

---

55    O'Sullivan, *The Levelling*, 24.

56    Teresa Ghilarducci, "Most Americans Don't Have a Real Stake in the Stock Market," *Forbes*, August 31, 2020. https://tinyurl.com/utt3mv2w.

57    Peter G Peterson Foundation, "Here's Everything the Federal Government Has Done to Respond to the Coronavirus so Far," March 15, 2021. https://www.pgpf.org/blog/2021/03/heres-everything-congress-has-done-to-respond-to-the-coronavirus-so-far.

4.6 percent of all wealth.[58] Such wealth disparity is concerning. Former president Teddy Roosevelt was also concerned about such a divide when he said, "Disaster will follow when two sections, or two classes, are so cut off from each other that neither appreciates the other's passions, prejudices, or indeed, point of view."[59]

Most conservatives would respond to information about generational wealth disparity without much surprise or concern. It has been common in free societies throughout history for the youngest generation to struggle financially until time and effort eventually results in that generation freeing themselves from their struggle. In the past, that transition was accomplished by an individual gaining experience or adding to their education. However, in comparison to previous generations, millennials face very different economic conditions. While Americans are more productive than they have ever been, overall output is unchanged. The United States is producing the same amount of products and services with fewer workers. This is different from what happened from 1947 to 1972 when productivity increased by almost 50 percent, but the United States produced twice as much to offset the effect added productivity had on unemployment.[60]

Globalism has also altered the economic conditions faced by millennials. Globalism has been an economic and job boon for many countries. Globalism doubled the number of workers in China, India, and the

---

58    Alicia Adamczyk, "Millennials own less than 5% of all U.S. Wealth," make it, October, 9, 2020. https://www.cnbc.com/2020/10/09/millennials-own-less-than-5percent-of-all-us-wealth.html.

59    Doris Kearns Goodwin, *Leadership: In Turbulent Times* (New York: Simon & Schuster, 2018), p. 38.

60    Oren Cass, *The Once and Future Worker* (New York: Encounter, 2018), p. 60.

Soviet block when those countries entered the world economy.[61] However, Americans have paid the price for the job growth in other countries, as globalism eliminated many middle class jobs in the United States. As a share of overall employment, there are now more high-end jobs for professionals and managers as well as more low-paid workers like teachers aids, waiters, janitors, and hairdressers. Those increases sandwich the loss of mid-level jobs, like administrative assistants, sales people, and production workers. Unfortunately, wages for high- and low-end jobs have not increased equally. Wages for the high-end professionals and managers have soared relative to the low-wage workers.[62]

The loss of middle-class jobs is felt household by household but also town by town. When a way of life vanishes and communities crumble as entire industries flee to other countries, those jobs are not easily replaced. When self-sufficiency gives way to dependency, cultural norms shatter. Families fail to form, adults and children are left adrift, and growth stops. Work is meaningful—not only because of what it means for the self-esteem and confidence of the person performing it, but also by what it provides to a family and what it does for a community.

The combination of technology, globalism, and concentration of power have created tremendous wealth, especially for the ownership class of this country. In free, capitalist societies such as the United States, the concentration of wealth in a narrow class of people may reach a point where the strength of the many poor rivals the strength in ability of a few rich. When that unstable equilibrium generates a critical situation, history deals with it either through legislation that redistributes wealth

---

61    Haskel and Westlake, *Capitalism Without Capital*, 124.

62    Susskind, *World Without Work*, 35.

or by revolution redistributing poverty.[63] Right now, Americans are in the midst of trying the former to avoid being forced into the latter. We are in a constant class struggle to redistribute the wealth accrued by the haves for the benefit of the have-nots. Debates about the level of taxation on income, capital, property, fuel, or retail sales go on without end. Calls for greater charity, better welfare, higher minimum wage, and more public services are all a means of transferring more income and wealth from the people who have it to the people who don't.

Income and wealth do not make people happier, although a lack of income and wealth can bring about considerable unhappiness. What higher income and wealth do offer is greater freedom. Those with more income and wealth have greater control over their time and have the luxury to pass their wealth on to future generations.

Consistent with that notion, the spending habits of the top 1 percent of income and wealth earners have changed. Conspicuous consumption on items such as second homes, cars, and jewelry has been replaced by inconspicuous consumption of non-visible, expensive goods and services that give those with great wealth more time and, over the long term, more opportunities. These include things like better education and healthcare, child care, nannies, housekeepers, and retirement savings.[64]

Educational spending is the biggest divide between the spending habits of the haves and have-nots. The wealthiest 1 percent spend 860 percent more on education than the average American.[65] The wealthy understand the importance of education in a world that values knowledge above all

---

63    Will Durant, *The Lessons of History* (New York: Simon & Schuster, 1968), loc. 602, Kindle.

64    Elizabeth Currid-Halkett, *The Sum of Small Things: A Theory of the Aspirational Class* (Princeton, NJ: Princeton University Press, 2017), p. 26.

65    Currid-Halkett, *The Sum of Small Things*, 70.

other capital. In his book, *The Conservative Sensibility*, author George Will points out that as the acquisition and manipulation of information becomes the greatest determinant of success, those with more aptitude via education and socialization accrue greater benefits.[66] Two centuries ago, wealth was determined by the amount of land one owned. One century ago, it was determined by the amount of large capital one owned. Today, the distinctive source of wealth is knowledge and information.

Even with free public education, there is only so much that can be done to augment those with less ability and level the playing field for education as a determinant of wealth.[67] Each year, America's 3.5 million high school seniors go in one of five directions. One-fifth do not complete high school. One-fifth graduate but do not get further education. One-fifth enroll in college but don't finish. One-fifth complete college but take a job that doesn't require a college education, and the final one-fifth successfully complete college and go on to a career requiring that degree.[68] College enrollment has increased significantly in the past two decades, but bachelor degree attainment hasn't changed at all. The percentage of 25 year olds with a bachelor's degree was actually less in 2015 than it was in 1995.[69] Despite tremendous effort by parents, teachers, scholarship donors, and employers, it has been difficult to get more than 90 percent of a country's residents to graduate from secondary school and more than 50 percent to graduate from college. This has been true across multiple cultures.[70]

---

66    George F. Will, *The Conservative Sensibility* (New York, Boston: Hachette, 2019)

67    George F. Will, *The Conservative Sensibility*, 343.

68    Cass, *The Once and Future Worker*, 102.

69    Cass, *The Once and Future Worker*, 106.

70    Susskind, *World Without Work*, 102.

The one-third of Americans who have obtained a college degree have accrued most of the benefits of the past few decades of economic growth.[71] But even within that one-third of Americans, children of the top 1 percent of income earners dominate the list of enrollees in the most elite schools. Of the top thirty-eight schools in the United States, there are more students from families in the top 1 percent of income earners than there are from the bottom 60 percent combined.[72]

Differences in the quality of education between the haves and the have-nots is accelerating. Those with disposable income are able to provide individual instruction, tutors, and summer camps for their children. The added level of customized instruction is very valuable. Students who get one-on-one instruction outperform 98 percent of kids in a traditional classroom.[73] While there is solid evidence that good teachers and good schools boost student achievement in a traditional classroom, nobody knows how to replicate those good teachers and good schools. This makes it nearly impossible to provide high-quality primary education evenly across the country. Redistributing some income and wealth by improving K–12 education in the United State is a perfectly laudable goal, but an inability to replicate good teachers and good schools means improving achievement scores and college preparedness broadly is unlikely in the future.[74]

---

71  Ben Sasse, *Them: Why We Hate Each Other—and How to Heal* (New York: St. Martin's Griffin, 2018), p. 32.

72  Greg Lukianoff and Jonathan Haidt, *The Coddling of the American Mind: How Good Intentions and Bad Ideas Are Setting Up a Generation for Failure* (New York: Penguin, 2018), p. 158.

73  Susskind, *World Without Work*, 158.

74  Oren Cass, *The Once and Future Worker*, 106.

Just like wealth, the fruits of education are handed down from one generation to the next and impact children before they even go to school. Among the less educated, parents rate obedience as more important than self-reliance by a factor of four to one. Amongst the well educated, those numbers are reversed. The words parents use to talk to their children are also different. Amongst the professional class, children hear eight times more encouraging words as discouraging ones, while children of welfare families hear only half as many encouraging words as discouraging ones.[75]

Self-reliance is to obedience what power is to subservience. It is a completely different lens from which to experience the world. Feelings of self-reliance and power come from a place deep inside where people feel capable of projecting themselves into the world in ways that will make a difference. They display a sense of purpose. For Americans in the back row, consigned to a worker class with invisible boundaries guarded by the ownership class, that sense is missing, and those without a sense of purpose become easy to control. They are more prone to believe simple messages from charismatic populist leaders at the political extremes that make complex problems sound like they have clear causes and simple solutions. Obedience and subservience are not only the path of least resistance but perhaps the only path available for those without self-reliance and power.

The result of living in the back row indefinitely can be humiliating. Good jobs once available right out of high school that provided financial stability have gone to Mexico, China, Central America, and Southeast Asia. The churches that offered a sense of community are cast as irrational and backward. The communities that offered a sense of pride

---

75    Paul Collier, *The Future of Capitalism* (New York: Penguin Random House, 2018), p. 113.

are dying. Into that vacuum come drugs and other forms of escape. Without familiar points of reference to offer perspective, good people can be convinced that a lack of purpose is their fault because they did poorly in school, are dumb, undisciplined, or unfocused. And it's not just them. This failure extends to their friends, families, and congregations. Everyone they know must be lazy, weak, and unmotivated or else they wouldn't be in this situation.

Such humiliation can be isolating. Lurking deep within even the most civilized of us is the same basic fear of being alone, unsupported, and exposed to danger. Even though we are very dispersed as a society, we still have the same need to be part of a group, to feel supported and protected on all sides. Cut people off from their group—make them feel alone and vulnerable—and you weaken them enormously.

We live in a world that seems more and more beyond our control. Our livelihoods are at the whim of global forces. The economic and environmental problems we face cannot be overcome by ourselves. A natural response when we feel overwhelmed is to retreat into various forms of passivity. If we don't try too much in life, we limit our circle of action. We can give ourselves the illusion of control. The less we attempt, the less chance for failure. If we make it look like we are not responsible for our individual fate, then our apparent powerlessness is more palatable. For this reason, it becomes attractive to retreat into certain narratives: it is genetics that control us, we are a product of our time, the country is run by billionaires, or nobody cares what I think.

From 1975 to 1999, the number of times that Americans annually entertained at their home went from fourteen to eight.[76] In 1990, the average American had between three and four deep meaningful

---

76    Sasse, *Them: Why We Hate Each Other,* 26.

friendships. Today it is less than two, a reduction of 50 percent.[77] Notably, this is especially true for men. Most male friendships come from work, and work is becoming a place with far less permanence. In the 1970s, the average person stayed at a job for 2.5 decades. Today it is four years.[78] Millennials born between 1980 and 2000 had an average of seven jobs in their twenties, and 60 percent changed careers at least once.[79] Men, unlike women, tend to stop forming new friendships once they marry or have children. By age 65, two-thirds of men say their wife is their best friend, but only one-third of women say the same thing.[80] Most men have atrophying relationships for decades prior to retirement and replace very few of them.

The most common way to handle humiliation and loneliness is to find a sense of pride wherever possible. Becoming a valued member of something larger than oneself is a first step. Jobs, churches, schools, and the communities they dwell in served as that "something" for decades. Communities without stable jobs, faith, and pride become fertile ground for other less desirable "somethings." Drug traps and meth labs have no membership requirements but offer a sense of inclusion. All you have to do is use. A child offers instant meaning and an immediate source of pride for young parents—even if the time, money, or resources to care for the child are lacking. Racial identity groups don't have a membership requirement—other than being born—and come with the built-in benefit of blaming other racial groups for problems that are beyond their control. When you have nothing, respect means everything.

---

77    Sasse, *Them: Why We Hate Each Other*, 81.

78    Sasse, *Them: Why We Hate Each Other*, 48.

79    Linda Kaplan Thaler and Robin Koval, *Grit to Great* (New York: Penguin Random House, 2015), loc. 627, Kindle.

80    Sasse, *Them: Why We Hate Each Other*, 81.

For many, America is not a place where they can find the respect they seek. It is a culture that selectively recognizes economic forms of value—a culture that preferentially values the credentials of education and the spoils that go with it. It is a meritocracy that allows anyone, regardless of race, gender, or culture, to rise to the top, provided they check the right boxes for education, internships, jobs, and home zip code. It follows a path that requires knowledge about how to apply and where to go for help that few, without the right family or the right community support, can successfully navigate. Even for those that do, the end of the path is a place with a very narrow definition of success.

This was not the future many had in mind at the dawn of the internet era in the early 2000s. The internet was going to decentralize power and create a nonhierarchical online world that would be different from the real world where power, money, and influence were entrenched. But as control over the internet has become the province of large corporate and political entities, our online experiences are being shaped in the same way and by the same entities as in real life. Amazon's algorithm, more than any one person, determines what books are read in the world today. Large media companies may not control what you think, but their decisions on which stories are newsworthy control what you think about. Social media directs your attention to stories, pictures, and videos that are designed to engage and enrage, drawing your eyes to websites with people who supposedly think and act just like you. It is in these safe, virtual spaces of like-minded people where influence is exerted and hate festers. The internet was supposed to distribute political power more widely. Although democracy distributes power amongst the people and anyone can run for public office, it is also true that it is very hard to win an election without access to the aristocrat class of donors and lobbyists. As a result, American democracy has tended toward dynasties like the Clintons, Kennedys, and Bushes.

We have come to defend an odd notion in this country that giving money to political campaigns is the equivalent of free speech. The consequence is that rich people have more free speech and thus more power than poor people. The more the government influences the flow of money through larger state and federal budgets, the more money is spent on elections.

Individual political donors give money as a means of expression. The flow of money to a party or a particular candidate is an outward signal of our internal political identity. It shows others whose team we're on and that our words and behavior are consistent. Institutional donors give money for an entirely different reason. Institutional money is given to a party or a particular candidate as a form of investment. Individual donors are polarizing. Institutional donors are corrupting. Individual money grabs headlines, but institutional money influences the transactions and regulations that matter.

The larger the political donation, the greater the influence. Small donations—less than $200—do not have to be reported to the Federal Election Commission. Typically, small donations make for good press by making the candidate's campaign appear organic and spread wide, but big donations get candidates elected and reelected. The 2016 presidential election was unusual in that regard. That year, Donald Trump, the first populist presidential candidate since Ross Perot, a generation earlier, raised $239 million from people donating $200 or less, just over one-third of the total amount of money he raised in that election but more than Bernie and Hillary combined and more than Obama in 2012.[81]

---

81    Eitan Hersch, *Politics Is for Power: How to Move Beyond Political Hobbyism, Take Action, and Make Real Change* (New York: Simon & Schuster, 2020), p. 80.

Trump's presidential candidacy aside, big dollar donations dominate House and Senate campaigns. Nearly half of all donations come from individuals giving more than $200.[82] Larger donations come from a handful of people, with less than 2 percent of all Americans donating to political campaigns at that level.[83]

Most large donors in political elections believe strongly in some issue. As a result, large donations don't go to moderate candidates. The political reach of large donors can extend beyond their own state when they find a candidate who can fall in line with their strongly held beliefs. In 1990, 69 percent of the money for a typical congressional race came from donors within the state. In 2012, 68 percent of the money for congressional races came from out of state.[84] Out of state donors tend to be more ideologically driven and can shift politicians to extreme positions. Consequently, we get a Congress of extremes, such as Rep. Alexandria Ocasio-Cortez on the left and Rep. Matt Gaetz on the right. More importantly, just like economic power divides us into haves and have-nots, political power does as well. When the politicians representing you and the large donors that support them are members of a club you can't afford to join, feelings of hate solidify and undermine the trust that Americans have in the political system.

The term trust has a common root with the word truth. A generation ago, trust within American culture came much easier because the truth was not so elusive. Newspapers, television, and radio could be trusted to report fact-intensive news. People who held themselves out as experts were trusted to be what they claimed to be.

---

82   "Small Donors Make Good Press, Big Donors Get You Elected," Open Secrets. https://www.opensecrets.org/resources/dollarocracy/04.php.

83   "Donor Demographics," Open Secrets.

84   Hersch, *Politics Is for Power*, 119.

Trust lowers the resistance within a culture. When we trust that the information we are given is reliable, trust that the food prepared for us is safe, trust that judges are impartial, or trust that our business associates will do what they say, it frees up our time and attention for other things. Over time, we have developed ingenious ways of building that trust with one another. Double entry accounting, peer review journals, and double-sourced eyewitness accounts enabled people across vast distances to interact regardless of cultural or religious boundaries without their honesty being doubted.

Functional cultures are able to place trust in people like accountants, journalists, physicians, scientists, government officials, and police officers. We trust that the reports, papers, and work that they do is an accurate representation of what actually happened. But today, fewer and fewer people trust that those professionals are independent. Their ability to represent the truth often feels more a result of self-interest than objective credentials. Their lack of trustworthiness makes them suspicious characters selling their version of the truth, and if that version turns out to be a lie, all the more reason to hate them and the group they represent.

It is interesting how some very wealthy people like Mark Cuban, Warren Buffett, Charlie Munger, or Peter Thiel are able to criticize institutions like the government, Wall Street, science, or the legal system with little repercussion. They are able to do so because they have a platform built on their fortunes and choose to speak for no one but themselves. They do not arrogantly claim to understand and speak for a larger group, only to people who choose to believe the same things they do. They are populists in their own right that can speak their truth because they don't need anything from us. In part, this explains the support for Donald Trump. His indifference to the political establishment was a rebellion against systems of representation that his supporters believe are no longer trustworthy. His victory was an unmasking of a political system full of cynics and hypocrites. From that perspective, the relationships between political representatives and constituents, between mainstream media and actual events, between science and reality, all feel like a scam. When trust in one elite group is lost, it tends to impact all of the group. Once people lose trust, they become less interested in the truth. Once the foundations of a political system are no longer viewed as credible, liars become tolerated or even admired.

The convergence of political, economic, and scientific authority into a technocratic cabal pushes public behavior to the extreme. It gives rise to populist movements like the alt-right or Antifa. There is a sense that those posing as experts are misleading, self-interested, and often use data that is fabricated to make their arguments more persuasive. Resentment by conservatives toward liberal universities and the progressive leadership of large cities is rooted in a sense that the technocratic haves are leading and governing for their own interests against the will of the have-nots. Experts and politicians can talk about things like unemployment or the environment, but they are not unemployed nor do they stop traveling in SUVs and private planes. Their constant predictions about impending doom dulls our sense of outrage and proportion. As members of the technocracy move in and out of politics and into well-paid private sector jobs, like lobbying, science, and consulting, it clarifies the line between the haves and have-nots, us and them, owners from the working class, elites from the commoners.

The populist idea that the nation needs reclaiming from the upper crust has echoes of the anti-colonial nationalism that sparked the Revolutionary War over 245 years ago. Perhaps that is where a glimmer of hope lies for the future. In the pre-Revolutionary War years, like-minded farmers and shopkeepers became energized by similar feelings of patriotism resulting in a rebellion against the British Empire. The feelings of patriotism come across in the Declaration of Independence, which asserted that the yoke of oppression would be cast aside and the source of power would come from the people. But revolutions and rebellions are not forms of governance, and the Declaration of Independence was not a document that could bind people together in a common culture in perpetuity. Six years after the end of the Revolutionary War, the Constitution was written as a protection against the people turning into a mob. It was a document for the public to control and regulate itself. The Declaration of Independence was about patriotism, classism, and anger, but the Constitution was about preserving the future.

That is a similar state we find our country in today. We have shown ourselves very capable of protesting and rioting, but eventually, we must refocus that energy into governing ourselves in a way that makes progress possible. Democracy is about checks and balances, constitutional restraints, and the sharing of power, not the concentration of power. Governance in a democracy is slow, grinding work. Democracies require negotiation, compromise, and concessions. Setbacks are inevitable, and victories are often partial.

The good news is that the tools for sustaining a democracy are more available to all of us than during any time in our history. Setting aside the issue of who is watching over those tools, connecting with others to create political influence has never been easier. Elon Musk has no more access to the internet than you or me. Jeff Bezos can speak to billions of people at once via social media, but so could anyone with the same amount of followers. The Bushes may be a political dynasty, but there are now many routes to political power. The Clintons came out of local government. Jimmy Carter came out of agriculture. Obama out of academia. Reagan out of Hollywood. An economically rich and diverse country fosters a strong civil society that offers many paths to political power. The internet has only compounded that fact and enabled those not in the ownership class to influence voters and win public office.

Another glimmer of hope is that the rate of concentration of wealth among a few is a natural result of the economic freedom permitted by morals and laws. Democracy allows the most liberty and thus accelerates concentration the most. That is not a statement to justify the status quo but rather an economic reality. Thus, the state of power inequality, economic inequality, and political inequality we find ourselves in is not the result of some malevolent, ill-minded people, but rather because we live in a country that permits and implicitly encourages the concentration of money and power. Moreover, what draws our attention when looking across our economic and political landscape are the relative differences between one group and another. When gross inequality is the general rule in a society, nothing stands out. Our mind accepts large differences in money and power between groups. But when everything is more or less level, the slightest variation becomes noticeable. Hence, the more equal men and women become, the more races mix with one another, the more success immigrants experience, the more we long for true equality. Longing is the fodder of envy, which fans the flame of hatred between dissimilar groups.

That is not to say that all our problems are small in comparison to problems of the past. We still battle demons from our recent history. While the Revolutionary War begat the Constitution and the foundation for treating each other with civility, civility did not ensue for all Americans. The Revolutionary War did not free African slaves, nor did the Industrial Revolution of the nineteenth century bring freedom and prosperity to them. Unlike every other country in the world, the United States had to fight a war for emancipation of the slaves, and even in the aftermath of the Civil War, our struggles with racism were just beginning. Decades of institutional racism, Jim Crow laws, and the tortured logic to justify the unequal treatment of an entire race ensued. Progress toward a nonracial distribution of economic and political power has been slow. Today, 26 percent of African Americans live in poverty compared to only 10 percent of whites. Five percent of white children will spend half their childhood in poverty, while 40 percent of African American children do the same.[85] The really hard question is to what degree is African American poverty due to past mistreatments versus contemporary ongoing racism. That is an issue that drives as much hate as any other and is the topic of the next chapter.

---

85    Michael D. Tanner, *The Inclusive Economy: How to Bring Wealth to America's Poor* (Washington, DC: The Cato Institute, 2018), p. 85.

# CHAPTER 4

★ ★ ★ ★ ★ ★ ★

# RACISM

As a white male author, writing about race makes me very uncomfortable. Physically, aesthetically, and behaviorally, I am unmistakably white. The words, sentences, and syntax I use to write this book undoubtedly reveal my ethnicity. I live in a predominantly white neighborhood in a predominantly white community and never have to explain why I prefer blue suits at work and cut-off T-shirts at home, keep my thinning hair short and straight, drive a four-wheel drive pickup, or prefer listening to hair metal and country music. In short, I never have to explain my whiteness.

I have, however, on occasion, felt the cruelty of racism expressed toward my Indian wife of twenty-eight years and our mixed-race Indian Caucasian children. In those moments, I did not care that the racist words aimed at us were being spoken by ignorant, small-minded people. All I felt was anger. I was not calm, curious, or empathetic. I had no desire to engage in a discussion to explore the underlying reason for their racist behavior. Every emotional impulse I had made me want them to hurt as much as they were hurting me and the people I love more than anyone else in the world.

These were not situations that brought out the best version of myself. But as angry as I felt during those moments, it would still be categorically untrue to say that I understand what it is like to be judged harshly by my race. For those who have experienced hatred based on their race, ethnicity, or skin color, I cannot empathize, but I think I can understand. From a non-white perspective, my writings on racism will seem akin to those of a reporter covering wartime battles. I can observe and analyze, but I'm not living in it. Nonetheless, in a book about why we have come to hate each other in this country, to not write about racism would be to ignore the elephant standing in the middle of the room.

Race matters. It has always mattered. It matters in all places and at all times. There is no country in the world that has avoided the conflicts that arise as humanity inevitably sorts itself into us and them based on skin color and culture. For high-minded liberal folks who think we might all be able to live together under some cosmopolitan, United Nations-type blended government, even a quick look at headlines from around the world makes such a thought seem naïve. On every continent, ethnic and racial fragmentation is a front page issue. Conflicts in the Balkans, Rwanda, Chechnya, Guyana, Australia, Iraq, Indonesia, India, and Israel are only some of the most well known. While humans are very social, our fatal flaw is that our affection is reserved for those we believe are similar to us in some way. Our desire to punish those that are not like us is stronger than our desire to please those that are like us.

In a sense, a focus on our differences is a paradox because we are so similar. There are approximately 20,000 human genes. Each of us, regardless of race, religion, size, shape, or color shares 99.9 percent of those genes with every other human being on the planet.[86] Somehow, we choose to ignore the obvious similarities of how we walk, digest our food, live together in families, hear in stereo, see in three dimensions, and spend the overwhelming majority of our time planning for the future. Instead, what draws our attention are differences. We notice the colors of skin and eyes, hair texture, preferred foods, the sports we cheer for, and the Gods we pray to. War, famine, and plagues have compelled humans to minimize differences temporarily in order to survive for brief periods of history, but as soon as the crisis is past, attention is refocused on the differences we believe make our particular group unique and special. Even if interracial marriage occurred on a grand scale over the next fifty generations and humanity blended together into one common color and ethnicity, we would somehow scramble to find new differences to divide those in our midst into us and them.

Similarities aside, much of the two and a half centuries of American history has been defined by how we have treated one another based on skin color, facial features, and hair texture. Four hundred years ago, African Americans were brought to the United States against their will to serve as slaves. This was well before the Revolutionary War and long before most whites voluntarily immigrated to the United States after 1840. Although the rest of the world may look at the United States as a country settled by white northern and western Europeans, in most cases African American families have been in the United States much longer. But we should forgive the rest of the world for their false impression. Despite their longer presence here, the United States has hardly been a

---

86    "Genetics vs. Genomics Fact Sheet," National Human Genome Research Institute, September, 7, 2018. https://www.genome.gov/about-genomics/fact-sheets/Genetics-vs-Genomics#:~:text=All%20human%20beings%20are%20 99.9,about%20the%20causes%20of%20diseases.

place where African Americans have held the upper hand of economic and political power.

Slavery was not unique to the United States. Slavery dates back to prehistorical times when humans first began living in cities. Prior to the formation of cities, when humans remained in small, hunter-gatherer tribes, there was no accumulation of wealth or division of labor. Survival of the tribe depended on constantly moving to get enough food to make it to the next season. However, with the dawn of agriculture and private property 10,000 years ago, large groups of unrelated people began to live together.[87] Cities formed, and the division of labor followed, since the entire tribe no longer needed to be involved in hunting and gathering the food necessary for survival. Tasks could be assigned or delegated, and thus control over labor became a symbol of power. Those who controlled a supply of free labor were especially powerful.[88] As some individuals accumulated wealth, others were enslaved to work for them. Slavery existed in prehistoric Egypt, Rome, pre-Columbian America, China, and Greece. During the Roman Empire, 35 percent of the population were slaves comprised of criminals, debtors, or prisoners of war. Most slavery was abandoned in Europe by the twelfth century and was replaced by serfdom, where the serfs were responsible for their own upkeep, saving the landowner money and labor costs.[89] But slavery persisted elsewhere. In the West African country of Mauritania, slavery

---

87 Rutger Bregman, *Humankind: A Hopeful History* (New York: Hachette, 2019), p. 243.

88 Byron Reese, *The Fourth Age: Smart Robots, Conscious Computers, and the Future of Humanity* (New York: Simon & Schuster, 2018), loc. 242, Kindle.

89 Timothy C. Winegard, *The Mosquito: A Human History of Our Deadliest Predator* (New York: Penguin Random House, 2019), p. 171.

wasn't outlawed until 1981 and, even then, had to be criminalized in 2007 because it was still being practiced.[90]

Slavery in the United States began in the seventeenth and eighteenth centuries with the desire for free labor in the tobacco fields. Half of all white Europeans who initially immigrated to the Caribbean and southern American colonies died from mosquito-borne illnesses, primarily malaria.[91] Africans, many of whom had built up immunity to malaria through the same genetic mutation that causes sickle cell anemia, became extremely valuable to landowners who were raising tobacco in the mosquito-infested lands of the Caribbean and the southern American colonies.

The first African slaves arrived in the American colonies on August 20, 1619, at the Jamestown colony after being kidnapped in Angola by Portuguese traders.[92] Between 1607 and 1627, 80 percent of all settlers of Jamestown died within the first year of their arrival. However, the profit margin on tobacco was 1,000 percent. Thus the Virginia company of England continued to send settlers, criminals, prostitutes, indentured servants, African slaves, and nearly anyone else they could find to continue the cultivation of tobacco.[93]

The appeal of free labor and the preservation of a culture with a clear distinction between owners and workers sustained slavery in the United

---

90    Ronald Bailey and Marian L. Tupy, *Ten Global Trends Every Smart Person Should Know: And Many Others You Will Find Interesting* (Washington, DC: Cato Institute, 2020), p. 102.

91    Winegard, *The Mosquito*, 180.

92    "First enslaved Africans arrive in Jamestown, setting the stage for slavery in America," History website, August 13, 2019. https://www.history.com/this-day-in-history/first-african-slave-ship-arrives-jamestown-colony.

93    Winegard, *The Mosquito*, 225.

States until 1865, when the world's only war ever fought over slavery finally ended. Sadly, the abolishment of slavery in the United States occurred thirty years after Britain, the former U.S. oppressor, did so itself.

At the end of the Civil War, there were 4.2 million former slaves, most of whom lived in the South. With their emancipation came a new struggle for equality. Formal laws legalizing slavery gave way to informal Jim Crow laws that prevented the next four generations of African Americans from voting, home ownership, quality education, and the accumulation of wealth. Although the Civil Rights Act of 1964 outlawed all forms of racial discrimination, the multigeneration loss of financial and educational opportunities dug a significant hole for African Americans born into the baby boomer (those born from 1946 to 1964) and Gen X (those born from 1965 to 1980) generations.

Educational capital, just like financial capital, is handed down from generation to generation. It takes time for subsequent generations to benefit from the investments made in education by their forebears. Those whose parents obtained a college degree are more likely to take challenging high school classes[94] as well as enroll and graduate from college.[95] This is not just a recent phenomenon. Half of Howard

---

94    Catherine Gewertz, "First-Generation College Students Face Challenges in High School Too," Education Week website, February, 8, 2018. https://www.edweek.org/teaching-learning/first-generation-college-students-face-extra-challenges-in-high-school-too/2018/02?cmp=soc-tw-shr.

95    Emily Forrest Cataldi, Christopher T. Bennett, and Xianglei Chen, RTI International, "First-Generation Students: College Access, Persistence, and Postbachelor's Outcomes," National Center for Education Statistics, February 8, 2018. https://nces.ed.gov/pubsearch/pubsinfo.asp?pubid=2018421.

University's African American graduates in 1940 were descended from a small group of slaves that were literate.[96]

Just like it takes time for the benefits of economic and educational investment handed down from prior generations to generate returns, it also takes time for beliefs and cultural attitudes to change. A culture that embraced slavery for 250 years did not change abruptly with the end of the Civil War. In 1870, the 15th Amendment was ratified, giving African Americans the right to vote. Shortly thereafter, Ellis Island became the entry point for hundreds of thousands of immigrants from Russia and eastern Europe, including Italians, Poles, Hungarians, Czechs, Serbs, Slovaks, and Greeks, along with non-Europeans from Syria, Turkey, and Armenia. The transcontinental railroad was completed, connecting the United States from east to west, and cities began to rapidly expand. People of different races and nationalities speaking diverse languages were compressed into the same neighborhoods and worked in the same factories. American culture evolved from a northern and western European dominance to a more worldly, less homogenous racial mixture.

The growing cultural complexity strained the limits of what new immigrants considered us and them. The Supreme Court's interpretation of the Equal Protection Clause of the 14th Amendment prohibiting states from denying "any person in its jurisdiction equal protection of the laws"[97] was a measure of racism in its complicated evolution at that moment. In 1896, members of the Supreme Court, only one generation removed from the Civil War, held in *Plessy v. Ferguson* that "separate but equal" was consistent with the Equal Protection Clause, making segregated schools permissible. But two generations later, in 1954, the

---

96    Tanner, *The Inclusive Economy*, 98.

97    "Interactive Constitution," National Constitution Center. https://constitutioncenter.org/interactive-constitution/amendment.

Court reversed the *Plessy* decision in *Brown v. Board of Education* and held that segregated schools were a violation of the Equal Protection Clause.[98] For Justices on the 1896 Court, who lived through the antebellum years, "separate but equal" represented progress. It was a decision that reflected their generation's current sense of racial relations. Equality was important in principle, as long as it wasn't taking place in your own backyard.

In comparison, Justices on the 1954 Court looked at separate but equal with the perspective of an additional five decades of African American oppression. Separate but equal to them had become legal cover for systemic racism. While the actual words of the 14th Amendment didn't change between 1896 and 1954, their meaning did. The fact that the meaning of words such as those in the 14th Amendment can change with historical context has become a significant source of hate between conservatives and liberals.

Even after school integration following the decision in *Brown v. Board of Education,* racism by whites against African Americans has persisted. The Supreme Court's decision was a historic change in federal law, but it was a change that took time to reverberate through a culture that now had over 300 years of racism behind it. In the ensuing ten years, Rosa Parks remained seated on a bus in Montgomery, Alabama, the National Guard forcibly desegregated schools in Little Rock, Arkansas, the Vietnam War began, and President Kennedy was assassinated. American culture evolved a bit further from the era of Jim Crow to a less racist, egalitarian mindset. In 1964, President Johnson pushed the Civil Rights Bill through Congress prohibiting discrimination based on race, color, religion, sex, or national origin for purposes of hiring, firing,

---

98    "Brown v. Board of Education," National Archives, Education Resources. https://www.archives.gov/education/lessons/brown-v-board.

or promoting.[99] The Civil Rights Bill was a turning point in American politics. Four-fifths of Republicans but only two-thirds of Democrats voted for the Civil Rights Bill. However, Democrats get credit for it because they were in the majority of the House and Senate and the presidency. That vote is remembered as the moment the South started to go Republican. Racial and social legislation began to fall along party lines. Southern conservatives now aligned with Republicans and liberals aligned with Democrats.[100]

The Civil Rights Bill may have outlawed discrimination, but racism isn't manifest in legal documents. Racism happens between real people who act out their beliefs and ideas in real life. The Nobel Prize winning physicist Max Planck made an insightful observation about how new ideas are adopted in a culture. In his autobiography, Planck wrote, "A new scientific truth does not triumph by convincing its opponents and making them see the light, but rather because its opponents eventually die and a new generation grows up that is familiar with it . . . another instance of the fact that the future lies with the youth."[101] Planck saw beyond a wide-eyed idealistic view of the world as he wanted it to be. He understood the realities of human emotion and the innate desire to see what we believe. Just like new scientific truths often rely on those with old beliefs to pass on, new ways of social thinking often become embedded in the culture only after an older generation passes the responsibility of leadership on to the next.

---

99    "Legal Highlight, The Civil Rights Act of 1964," U.S. Department of Labor, OASAM. https://www.dol.gov/agencies/oasam/civil-rights-center/statutes/civil-rights-act-of-1964#.

100    Klein, *Why We're Polarized*, 30.

101    Max Planck, *Scientific Autobiography and Other Papers*, trans. Frank Gaynor (New York: New York Philosophical Library, 1949), pp. 33, 97.

Racism didn't end with the Civil War, *Brown v. Board of Education*, or the Civil Rights Act. It continues despite the protests of the deaths of George Floyd, Jacob Blake, and Breonna Taylor. But with time, race relations have gotten better—not ideal, but better. As subsequent generations of Americans come into their own, immigration, births, and deaths grind away at the racial composition of the country. Today in the United States, seven out of ten seniors in the baby boomer generation are white and Christian, while fewer than three in ten young adults fit the same description.[102] The generational change plays its hand as Gen X and millennials have a different racial and religious composition. Their experiences are unique, creating different expectations regarding race relations than the generations that preceded them.

For example, in 1958, 44 percent of whites said they would move if a Black family became their next door neighbor.[103] Today in city after city, a map of racial change shows neighborhoods predominantly with people of color near downtowns growing whiter, while suburban neighborhoods that were once largely white are experiencing an increased share of Black, Hispanic, and Asian American residents.[104]

A mixing of races that occurs when living and working closely with one another has changed economic conditions for African Americans. The rate of poverty for African Americans was cut in half between 1966

---

102    Klein, *Why We're Polarized*, 104.

103    Abigail Thernstrom and Stephen Thernstrom, "Black progress: how far we've come and how far we have to go," Brookings Institute website, March 1, 1998. https://www.brookings.edu/articles/black-progress-how-far-weve-come-and-how-far-we-have-to-go/.

104    *New York Times.* https://www.nytimes.com/interactive/2019/04/27/upshot/diversity-housing-maps-raleigh-gentrification.html.

and 2019.[105] The percentage of African Americans completing college increased by a factor of six between 1962 and 2019.[106] The number of Black college and university professors more than doubled between 1970 and 1990; the number of physicians tripled; the number of engineers almost quadrupled; and the number of attorneys increased more than sixfold.[107]

But there is a long way to go. A 2014 study found that 75 percent of white people have no non-white friends.[108] In the decades since affirmative action was first instituted, the poverty rate for African Americans has remained significantly higher than white families, with 21 percent living below the poverty line in comparison to 9.6 percent of white families.[109] African Americans are 3.7 times more likely to be arrested for marijuana possession than whites, despite reporting similar levels of marijuana use.[110]

While our historical struggles with slavery, Jim Crow, and civil rights reflect the most explosive form of racism, racism isn't confined to African Americans and whites. This is the racism I am familiar with. Noticeably, the racist comments directed toward my Indian American mixed-race family that have hurt me the most were the ones I never saw coming. When I see the stars and bars or swastikas displayed alongside a group

---

105    Jack Horton, "George Floyd: How far have African Americans come since the 1960s?" BBC News. https://www.bbc.com/news/world-us-canada-52992795.

106    Horton, "George Floyd."

107    Thernstrom and Thernstrom, "Black progress."

108    Brittany Wong, "Why We Need More Close Interracial Friendships," HuffPost, September 4, 2020. https://www.huffpost.com/entry/close-interraacial-friendships_l_5f5122c8c5b6946f3eaed704.

109    "Poverty Rate by Race/Ethnicity," KFF, 2019. https://www.kff.org/other/state-indicator/poverty-rate-by-raceethnicity.

110    Tanner, The Inclusive Economy, 162.

of people, it is maddening, but at the same time, serves as a warning. The presence of racist symbols prepares my mind for the racist rants and behaviors that are likely to follow. But racism that comes from out of nowhere is like an uppercut that connects squarely on my chin. One day, while I was fixing the fence on our farm, some new neighbors from a rental house down the road approached me. After greeting each other, one of them expressed relief that a white man owned the farm since they had seen some "towelheads" working there earlier. I could immediately feel the heat of rage radiating from my flushed face as I squared my shoulders and gripped the pliers in my hand tight enough to turn my knuckles white. When I asked them in a deep, loud voice if they were referring to my wife, my children, or my in-laws, their eyes widened, and they began apologizing profusely. "I'm sorry sir, no disrespect" is what I heard, but I knew their real regret was being called out. In a not so neighborly tone, I reminded them that the food my family helped grow on our farm went to the local food bank to feed people who were hungry, regardless of their race. I told them that my wife treated women and delivered babies at the local hospital without any concern for their skin color, and that I would expect that she or any other non-white person that was ever on our farm would be treated with similar dignity and respect. After a much too long series of bumbling apologies, my new neighbors went on their way, but the edginess I feel every time I drive past their house never leaves. Thus, while I do not know what it's like to be judged harshly by my race, I can understand some of the anger that racism stirs among African Americans and immigrants.

The number of immigrants comprising the U.S. population has gone from 9 percent in 1990 to 14 percent in 2015.[111] While those

---

111    O'Sullivan, *The Levelling*, 50.

immigrants were born in over one hundred different countries,[112] 50 percent are Hispanic, which makes the immigrant population less diverse and assimilation less likely and adds another layer of complexity to race relations.[113]

The complexity of racial relations in the United States does not deter people of different races from all over the world from immigrating to the United States. Currently, there are over 4.7 million people waiting for one of about 366,000 annual permanent immigration visas.[114] Perhaps the reason so many are willing to wait so long is that ethnicity and language have not proven to be a barrier to success for many groups of new immigrants. Jews, Nigerians, Haitians, Indians, Persians, and East Asians have higher incomes and greater percentages of college and postgraduate degrees on a per capita basis than white people.[115] Their success has not been without struggle. Each of those ethnic groups has faced their own form of racism and oppression. Chinese Americans could not become U.S. citizens until 1943, Indian Americans in 1946, and other Asian Americans in 1952.[116]

---

112    "The nations represented within the United States," cartoMission. https://cartomission.com/2014/08/19/the-nations-represented-within-the-united-states/.

113    Robert D. Kaplan, *The Revenge of Geography* (New York: Random House, 2012), loc. 5274, Kindle.

114    David J. Bier, "Immigration Wait Times from Quotas Have Doubled: Green Card Backlogs Are Long, Growing, and Inequitable, Cato Institute, June 18, 2019. https://www.cato.org/publications/policy-analysis/immigration-wait-times-quotas-have-doubled-green-card-backlogs-are-long#current-wait-times-by-nationality.

115    Amy Chua and Jed Rubenfeld, *The Triple Package* (New York: Penguin, 2015), p. 238.

116    Mark W. Moffett, *The Human Swarm: How Societies Arise, Thrive and Fall* (New York: Basic Books, 2018), p. 364.

With those ethnic groups having so much success, it begs the question as to what degree African American social and economic struggles are due to past racism versus contemporary, ongoing racism. This is one of the most divisive political issues in the United States today. From the liberal Democratic view, poverty and lack of power in the African American community is a result of ongoing racism and the oppressive social structure within American culture. White people with money and power oppress and marginalize African Americans, thereby retaining their money and power. Further, since African Americans have less money and power, the deck is perpetually stacked against them. Liberal Democrats reject the idea that the world is a meritocracy and that the playing field can ever be level. In contrast, the conservative Republican view is that poverty and lack of power is a result of individual behavior. They reject the idea that systemic racism against African Americans exists or that inherent privilege for white people tips the playing field in their favor. If racism is the tinder for a political fire, an allegation of white privilege is the gasoline that turns the fire into an inferno.

Despite the economic success and growing political power of East Asians, Indians, Persians, Nigerians, and Haitians, those ethnic groups are rarely accused of the same level of racism or oppression against African Americans. Those accusations consistently fall to whites, particularly white males. Just like it is risky for a white male like me to write about racism, complaining about being falsely accused of racism is asking to be derided. The eye rolls from liberal Democrats are audible. How could a group that has been racist for 400 years propose to suddenly switch the narrative and complain about being falsely accused of racism? From the left's perspective, there is no intellectual turf on which that argument can live. The left's definition of racism is hatred by the powerful against the powerless on the basis of race. With those terms, there is no opportunity for conversation. The righteous speak. The sinners listen.

But regardless, if there is enough intellectual turf for white males to complain about false accusations of racism, there is no shortage of blame to place on white males for problems ranging from inequality to racism and climate change. Author Douglas Murray contends that the argument against white men is essentially an analysis of power. From the perspective of power, nothing else like love, charity, skill, integrity, or resilience is of consequence. Further, the people who wield the power do not derive it from production or results, but rather it is given to them because their race and color sit atop the societal food chain. The society is not only capitalist but patriarchal and racist.[117] Moreover, if some power can be squeezed out from those at the top of the food chain, it will necessarily trickle down to those on lower links of the chain, which is a good thing.

Arguments like this erode the individualism situated at the core of a democratic culture by defining people as a manifestation of only two characteristics. We are who we are based on race and sex rather than complex, self-defining participants full of both good and evil trying to find our way in a complicated, free society. The irony is that those who accuse white men of being the provenance of all things evil insist that accusers should be judged on their individual behavior, not just on the basis of their race or sex. In the excitement of defining their enemy, accusers fail to extend the same grace they afford themselves, based on the logic of revenge that it is time for the oppressors (or their progeny) to be oppressed.

The ground rules the accusers work from make any progress on racial relations grind to a halt, and accusations of racism run rampant. The finger-pointing for racist behavior goes in every direction since there

---

117   Douglas Murray, *The Madness of Crowds: Gender, Race and Identity* (London: Bloomsbury, 2019), loc. 976, Kindle.

is no dominant racial group today. Even though non-Hispanic whites comprise 60 percent of the U.S. population,[118] the deep political divide among white people makes one side culturally incomprehensible from the other. As a result, every racial group feels attacked, pitted against each other in a zero-sum game for jobs and spoils. Racist and ethnonationalist groups even borrow the language of minority rights and identity politics to protest that they are the new victims of racism. For example, in August of 2017, white supremacists marched through the streets of Charlottesville, Virginia, claiming "you will not replace us" and taking on the role of victim. The existential threats they say they fear sounded oddly similar to the messages of those marching for civil rights in the 1960s. The Charlottesville protestors denounced discrimination against white people, suppression of their First Amendment rights, maligning their cultural heritage, undermining their self-esteem, and a subjective desire to eliminate the white race.[119]

In the pursuit of anti-racism, we have turned race from one of many important issues into something that is more important than anything else. Black studies in universities across the country emphasize a particular version of culture, history, politics, and literature. Black studies have gone from celebrating Black culture to attacking those that are not Black, fostered by a liberal faculty who, at best, doesn't want to offend and, at worst, supports the attack. At NYU, the fallout between Black and white students reached the point where Black students requested separate dormitories from other students in order to create a "safe space" away from white students where they could feel free to

---

118    "Quick Facts," United States Census website. https://www.census.gov/quickfacts/fact/table/US/PST045219.

119    Olga Khazan, "How White Supremacists Use Victimhood to Recruit," *The Atlantic*, August 15, 2017. https://www.theatlantic.com/science/archive/2017/08/the-worlds-worst-support-group/536850/.

express themselves.[120] It's a confusing message to send to those of us that are not Black. How does one respond to "you must understand me!" when it is communicated simultaneously with "you cannot understand me!"? To their credit, the NYU administration denied the request, but it is hard to see the request as anything but a regression in racial relations.

It may be true that some African Americans are held back because of their race, but at a time in history when racial equality has never been better, oppression is portrayed by liberal Democrats as having never been worse. In 1994, 39 percent of Democrats and 26 percent of Republicans believed that the primary reason African Americans could not get ahead was because of racism. In 2017, 64 percent of Democrats believed that to be true, but only 14 percent of Republicans.[121] White liberals have moved so far to the left on race that they are now more to the left than the typical Black voter. White liberal Democrats are now less likely than Black voters to say that Black people should be able to get ahead without any special help.[122]

Minimizing differences between people with laws and policies may be a worthy societal aim, but pretending differences don't exist is to ignore reality. To assume that race means nothing would be ridiculous, but to assume it means everything will be fatal to the United States' survival as a sovereign entity. Simply honoring someone for their membership in a group is too simplistic. Respect is owed to individuals because of their humanity, not because of their membership in a group when that membership is simply conveyed by accident of birth. Honor should

---

120    "NYU: Implement Black Student Housing," Change.org petition. https://www.change.org/p/black-student-housing-at-nyu.

121    Klein, *Why We're Polarized*, 11.

122    Matthew Yglesias, "The Great Awakening," Vox, April 1, 2019. https://www.vox.com/2019/3/22/18259865/great-awokening-white-liberals-race-polling-trump-2020.

flow to individuals because of their display of moral excellence, such as honesty, integrity, or compassion, not because of membership in some group. Beliefs don't make you a better person, behavior does. Judging people by their actions, not by what they say or believe, is where the truth lies.[123]

If we are to continue the mixing of races and ethnicities in this country from around the world, time and understanding are needed. Ethnicities can be ingested into the whole, but it takes time. The melting pot has to simmer, not flash fry. The urge for immigrants to feel similar yet different ensures that low and slow is the right method for making sure everyone has time to congeal. Accusations of racism in cases where the evidence is thin doesn't make the melting pot simmer any faster; it only increases the chances of starting a fire.

Taking time and understanding the experiences of those of a race other than our own is essential, but developing empathy is exceedingly difficult. What we experience firsthand is always more compelling than what we learn second hand. We can read about or watch what others are going through, but our memories, beliefs, and expectations come from our own unique experiences. For example, in 2009, just after the recession, nationwide unemployment was 10 percent. For African American males aged sixteen to nineteen without a high school diploma, the unemployment rate was 49 percent. Caucasian females over the age of forty-five with a college degree at that time had an unemployment rate of 4 percent.[124] Depending on sex and race, one would recall that moment in history very differently. Similarly, a 2019 poll showed that

---

123    Robert Greene, *The 33 Strategies of War* (New York: Penguin, 2006), loc. 317, Kindle.

124    Morgan Housel, *The Psychology of Money: Timeless Lessons on Wealth, Greed, and Happiness* (Petersfield, United Kingdom: Harriman House, 2020), loc. 179, Kindle.

54 percent of whites think race relations are good, while only 40 percent of African Americans agreed.[125] "Good" is a matter of perspective.

Understanding cannot be compelled. When understanding is demanded so that disagreement is avoided and conversations that risk being offensive are taboo, understanding is no longer understanding. Rather, it is, as comedian George Carlin might have said, fascism pretending to be manners.[126]

Being compelled to speak or act in a certain way to hide one's beliefs is a source of hatred for many conservative Republicans. It is policing individual thought. It is determining an outcome, not based on the merit of an argument or the performance of good work but because of the actions of prior generations. It cuts to deeply held religious beliefs that many Republicans identify with, such as the biblical notions of getting what is deserved from Proverbs or reaping what is sown from Galatians.

Because political power tends to run a decade behind demographic changes, there is a lag between the cultural power a new generation feels and its translation to victories on election day. An older, whiter, more Christian, more Republican generation turns out to vote at higher rates but still feels dismissed and culturally offended by a younger, more racially mixed, less Christian, and more Democratic generation. While we continue to make progress with race relations, Republicans who feel their religious beliefs are mocked or dismissed while being held liable for the racist actions of prior generations layer on another level of hate toward liberals who claim to know better. That is the topic of the next chapter.

---

125    Bailey and Tupy, *Ten Global Trends*, 58.

126    George Carlin, *Brain Droppings*, (New York: Hachette, 1998)

# CHAPTER 5

★ ★ ★ ★ ★ ★ ★

# RELIGION

Religion was woven into the cultural fabric of my small, midwestern hometown. Fairbury, Nebraska, of the 1970s and 1980s was small enough to offer two degrees of separation between its citizens. Either the person passing me on the street was someone I knew or, at a minimum, knew someone I knew. Most of the time, I could say three things about the passing person with confidence: where they lived, where they worked, and what church they attended. The church you attended said a lot about both what you believed and who your friends were. In my family, church was the hub of our social activity.

Sunday mornings in Fairbury were the time to put on "church clothes." For the men and boys, that meant sport coats, ties, and freshly shined shoes. For the women and girls, it meant dresses, heels, makeup, and jewelry. Most families parked their car in the same place each Sunday and sat in the same church pew, making the job of ushering mostly ceremonious. Greeters at each door handed out bulletins, children lit candles, and pipe organ music played. When the service commenced, colorfully cloaked choirs walked in followed by the minister in a black robe and brightly hued sash. As a congregation, we stood and sat on cue, sang together, chanted together, prayed together, recited our mutual beliefs, and took part in religious rituals that had been practiced for generations. At the time, I put very little thought into why these rituals were performed or what they meant. What I did know was that the people in our congregation were part of my family's inner circle. They were people that we visited in the hospital when they were sick, whose sidewalks and driveways we helped clear of snow in the winter, who we called to congratulate when good fortune looked their way, and who we took food to when someone in their family died. We were connected to one another by a similar faith, but more so by a mutual caring for one another.

For better or worse, as I have grown older and moved from my hometown, I attend church less and read more. Years of studying math, physics, chemistry, anatomy, and physiology for engineering and medical degrees made the world around me less mysterious. I now understand that planets orbit the sun and objects fall to earth, not because God wills it, but rather because the space around them is curved by a gravitational field. Plagues and pestilence are not the wrath of God but the result of novel bacteria and viruses that infect their human hosts. Darwin's explanation of the origins of the five biological kingdoms comes with a lot more compelling evidence than the story of Noah. As science explains mysteries, religion has fewer gaps to fill. As science grows, faith wavers. That fact makes this a scary time to be alive for many people.

Humans have a deep need to believe in something. For all of recorded history, that "something" has been religion. Christianity and Judaism in the Americas and Europe; Islam in Africa and the Middle East; Hinduism in India; and Buddhism, Taoism, and Confucianism in

Eastern Asia became the dominant religions of the world over the past 4,000 years. But as long-standing religious beliefs make less logical sense and doubt creeps in, we get a little crazy. Without a unifying belief to anchor us, calm us, and give us courage, we become tribal and latch on to any small group that gives us a sense of belonging.

Religion has organic beginnings. Its compelling proposition is to explain the unexplainable and soothe the ultimate fears of death and suffering. Religion can take those fears and transform them into more manageable emotions that make sacrifice for the well-being of others possible. All of the world's great religions teach believers that the things they are afraid of are going to happen, but there is no need to be afraid. The reassurance of an inevitable but peaceful transition from life to death can be heard in the oft-repeated Psalm 23:4, "Yea, though I walk through the valley of the shadow of death, I will fear no evil: for thou art with me."[127]

Religious belief became the foundation for governance. The common moral code of all enduring religions is a combination of truth, compassion, equality, freedom, courage, and responsibility.[128] It's a formula that has enjoyed remarkable success. There is no significant example in all human history of a society successfully maintaining the moral life of its people without the aid of religion.[129] Even in communist countries that prohibit the practice of religion, the government merely replaces the church as the vendor of comfort and hope.

---

127    Psalm 23:4 (King James Bible)

128    Yuval Noah Harari, *21 Lessons for the 21st Century* (New York: Penguin Random House, 2018), p. 208.

129    Durant, *The Lessons of History*, loc. 548.

Religion has been the great unifier of societies. Social order does not simply rise from the earth like a vine, winding its way through the masses to establish civil harmony. Social order and hierarchy are created in cities, states, and nations from ideas that spring from the minds of human creators. Social order and hierarchy are not self-sustaining and require a constant infusion of thought and energy to be sustained. Thus, social order is fragile. The larger and more complex the society, the more energy and thought is required and the more fragile it becomes. Politicians and leaders have leaned on religion to establish and sustain social order. Religion adds the crucial role of divine legitimacy to laws and edicts. It contends that the laws governing their people are not the result of human caprice but rather are ordained by a supreme authority. Making laws the province of the divine means that adherence to those laws is a pious act, thereby ensuring social stability.[130]

Religion propels believers to be generous, not because religious people are more devout or more saintly, but rather because they perceive a higher purpose in the close kinship with other religious practitioners. Friendships and group activities are mixed in with the shared morality of religion, creating generosity. We learn to live, trade, and trust with others who share a common moral code. When members of a community lose that common moral code, people are less happy, less efficient, and less trusting of one another.[131] Only recently are there examples of societies trying to function without a common religious moral code. The sustainability of those societies is questionable. Predominant atheist societies in Europe have existed for less than fifty years and are among

---

130    Yuval Noah Harari, *Sapiens: A Brief History of Humankind* (New York: Harper Collins, 2015), p. 210.

131    Haidt, *The Righteous Mind,* 312,

the least effective at turning their resources into prosperity and progeny, making their long-term survival suspect.

Religion is not hard to sell. For many, there is a deep genetic desire for religious faith and belief. The Minnesota Twin Study of Adult Development began in 1986 to identify how nature and nurture interact to cause individual differences. Its researchers primarily conduct personality and interest tests with more than 8,000 twin pairs and family members to understand the role genetics and environment play in personality and mental development.[132] One of their studies looked at identical twins separated at birth and raised apart from one another. The study analyzed how genetics and environment influenced something called religiousness, a measure of religious devotion. The study found that 47 percent of religiousness is genetic. Only 11 percent of religiousness came from the influence of the surrounding environment. In other words, genetics plays a much greater role than environment in determining how religious one becomes.[133] The corollary to that observation is that morals have a genetic component, and it is those morals that shape our religion, not the other way around.[134] We are born with an innate sense of right and wrong, fairness, empathy, compassion, and self-sacrifice.[135] This intrinsic quality of religion makes it a part

---

132    "Other Twin Research at the U of M," Minnesota Center for Twin and Family Research, October 20, 2021. https://mctfr.psych.umn.edu/research/UM%20research.html.

133    Jim Davies, *Riveted: The Science of Why Jokes Make Us Laugh, Movies Make Us Cry, and Religion Makes Us Feel One With the Universe* (New York: Martin's Press, 2014), p. 17.

134    Davies, *Riveted*, 235.

135    Emily Esfahani Smith, "As Babies, We Knew Morality," *The Atlantic*, November 18, 2013. https://www.theatlantic.com/health/archive/2013/11/as-babies-we-knew-morality/281567/.

of every culture regardless of social or economic development. Only language, tool making, and art can make a similar claim.[136]

Religion fits well with the lifestyle of people living in prosperous nations. Religious people are healthier than the nonreligious. Religious prayer and meditation help manage negative emotions, reduce stress, lessen panic under pressure, and lower blood pressure. Religious people exercise more, smoke less, drink less, have more friends, get married more often, and lead a longer life.[137]

Religion solves another important problem for cities, states, and nations. It gets people who do not and never will know each other to sacrifice and cooperate. Despite a lack of familial connection, religion sets the stage for complete strangers to "imagine that they imagine" the same city, state, or nation. The worship of a God helps communities cohere, succeed, and outcompete others. Religions also help people achieve together what would be impossible on their own. The use of religion in fighting wars is evident throughout history, dating back to the Crusades. The First Crusade in the eleventh century, conceived to take back the Holy Lands from Muslims, was made possible by the coordination of a remarkable 80,000 European Christians who professed the same beliefs and marched from Europe to Jerusalem to prove it. More recently, the phrase "For God and Country" is used by U.S. military groups, including the American Legion, as a rallying cry to summon courage before battle and as a reminder of the reason for service. The same phrase

---

136    Davies, *Riveted,* 18.

137    Davies, *Riveted,* 233.

also served as the confirmation signal by Navy SEALs during the raid on the compound where Osama bin Laden was killed.[138]

Religion has been essential to the successful development of humanity on every continent. However, development has come at a price. The religious dualism of good and evil, light and dark, divine and demonic creates a context for quickly dividing people into us and them. Using a religious force that binds people together with a common moral code glorifies one group while marginalizing or even vilifying those that are not in the group. Religion, above all else, is interested in the creation and maintenance of order. It preserves a social structure, but not while searching for the truth. A search for truth weakens religion. Religion is powerful when believers submit to the will and common good of a religious group, but is weakened by factions that question those beliefs. Adherence to a common meaning of the stories, parables, and even individual words of the religion binds believers together, provided the stories and beliefs are absolute and beyond inquiry. The illogic of religion's explanations for the creation of life, meaning, suffering, and redemption is not a weakness but its essential strength.

Common religious practices help groups outcompete nonreligious groups. Religious groups have better cohesion and are more likely to survive than groups that are less cohesive.[139] This has given them a reproductive advantage and an enhanced ability to pass on religious genes to subsequent generations.[140] The survival advantage was assisted by a longstanding religious norm to care for the sick. Unlike the pagan

---

138    Nicholas Schmidle, "Getting Bin Laden," *The New Yorker*, August 8, 2011.

139    Haidt, *The Righteous Mind,* 305.

140    Haidt, *The Righteous Mind,* 294.

religions of ancient Greece and Rome, Christianity, in particular, spoke to the sanctity of life. The ill were nursed back to health, which drew more people to the Christian religion as malaria, tuberculosis, leprosy, influenza, smallpox, and other diseases first appeared. The concern for life, along with Christian charitable practices, fostered a sense of belonging and community that in turn encouraged closer trade and business relationships between Christians.[141]

Ironically, it was respect for the sanctity of life that began to undermine religious faith. As plagues and pandemics took large numbers of lives, particularly the black plague of the fourteenth century, which killed one-third of all Europeans, religious followers began to question the protection and salvation religion promised.[142] Christian priests and bishops died while caring for the sick. Monasteries and local parishes emptied. Several generations later, Martin Luther and the Protestant Reformation fractured the Catholic monopoly on Christianity and created space for new ideas and alternative explanations to traditional Vatican teaching.

The Reformation coincided with the beginning of the scientific revolution and greater public literacy. Answers to questions about the origin of mankind; the relationship of the earth, sun, and stars; and sickness, death, and the afterlife were no longer the exclusive province of priests and bishops. Answers came from observation and experimentation, which could be widely shared and understood through the written word. Nicolaus Copernicus formulated a model of the universe placing

---

141    Winegard, *The Mosquito*, 106.

142    Olivia Fox Cabane and Judah Pollack, *The Net and the Butterfly: The Art and Practice of Breakthrough Thinking* (New York: Penguin Random House, 2017), p. 64.

the sun rather than the earth in the center.[143] Galileo Galilei spent the last nine years of his life under house arrest for following the position of Copernicus against the wishes of the Catholic Church.[144] Slowly, a revolution in mathematics, physics, astronomy, biology, anatomy, and chemistry led by giants, such as Isaac Newton, Francis Bacon, Robert Boyle, and Johannes Kepler, began to explain natural phenomena that were previously left to the mystery of religion. The progression of scientific knowledge continued through the nineteenth and twentieth centuries as Charles Darwin, Marie Curie, Albert Einstein, and Nikola Tesla left fewer gaps for religion to fill, further undermining the stories and myths that had held societies together for thousands of years.

The scientific revolution and the ensuing centuries of scientific reflection in correlation with the receding role of religion have created a modern political problem that has yet to be solved. Just as it was in my hometown, religion was the source of social cohesion, cooperation, generosity, and the motivation for self-control. Without religion as the firm foundation of those morals and standards, what replaces it? The answers thus far have been less than satisfying.

One response has been to create natural law religions such as liberalism, conservatism, communism, capitalism, or nationalism. These are political ideologies, but at their core is a belief that a particular way of thinking is summoned by a higher power and can serve as an alternative source of morals and values. Natural law religions have rules and protocols created and enforced by the majority in control with little

---

143    Christopher M. Linton, *From Eudoxus to Einstein: A History of Mathematical Astronomy* (Cambridge: Cambridge University Press, 2004).

144    Rachel Hilliam, *Galileo Galilei: Father of Modern Science* (New York: The Rosen Publishing Group, 2005), p. 96.

room for individual variation and expression. Money is the common denominator of success, which makes morality fluid and definable by those with money.

Another response has been to invest more in education to create a greater number of people with a deeper understanding of science, business, and human behavior. However, the more resources invested in education, the more stratified a society becomes. When that happens, efforts must be made to instill some commonalities amongst disparate groups of people. Otherwise, shared values become attenuated, and there is less to bind a country together.[145] To double down on education and science as a substitute for religion is to pit one against the other. The pursuit of new scientific knowledge through education and research is ultimately a pursuit of power. Through that pursuit, science has created the remarkable ability to fight wars, cure disease, and produce food, all things that at one time were the purview of religion. A competition between education and religion for the soul of society is a zero-sum game that results in weakening both.

That competition has resulted in a standoff between one political group and another. Religious conservative Republicans on one side and nonreligious liberal Democrats on another. White evangelical Protestants prefer the Republican Party 3 to 1 over the Democratic Party, while religiously unaffiliated voters now lean Democrat by 2.5 to 1 over Republican.[146] Non-spiritual Democrats are fixated on the illogic and dark side of religion, while religious Republicans fear the moral

---

145    Will, *The Conservative Sensibility*, 361.

146    Thomas Edsall, "In God We Divide," *The New York Times*, March 25, 2020. https://www.nytimes.com/2020/03/25/opinion/religion-democrats-republicans. html.

vacuum left by religion's absence. Republicans are mocked for their Bible-waving, while Democrats wave the rebellious flag of liberalism, rationality, and social change irrespective of morals, governance, and respect for individuals.

Those who dismiss religions as fossilized philosophies neglect the fact that religions often do what political ideology rarely does—set in motion cascading events. Intangibles like religious faith have historical heft. Without religion to make sacrifice sacred, people think of most decisions in terms of cost and benefit. Societies with that ethos fail. Even if religion cannot be rationally justified, it is practically justifiable because people who follow religious rules preserve social order. Believing in religion may be irrational, but it got us into functional societies. Creating a secular society would be to try and outwit evolution. That is a tall order. Religion may not be the only way to get people to behave well in a community, but it's what we have used for 4,000 years.[147]

The irrationality of religion is not without benefit. In a study of competitive athletes, those that were more honest and didn't deceive themselves about their talent tended to perform worse in competition. Good luck charms increase performance by up to 50 percent. Even though rational thought might be a worthy aspiration, if your goal is happiness or success, rationality might not be your best play.[148]

The growing vacuum of morals and values has been coupled with the ability to communicate from one to everyone via the internet and social media. The vertical lines of communication between generations have been replaced with horizontal peer-to-peer attachments that can span

---

147   Davies, *Riveted,* 231.

148   Davies, *Riveted,* 233.

the globe but, paradoxically, exist within ever-narrower channels. Rather than a clash of civilizations, we are getting a collapse of communities.[149] Today, a farmer in Fairbury may share more in common with a farmer in Fargo than with their neighbors that shared the same church pew a generation before. Religion once united us, now the internet divides us. Shared morals and values are important, but fellowship and friendship is missing. As much as farmers in Fairbury and Fargo may have in common with one another, they have never sung together, chanted together, prayed together, recited their mutual beliefs in unison, sat in a hospital room, or brought dinner to one another when a family member died.

Karl Marx called religion "the opium of the masses." He meant that religion provided the answers that could stop people from asking questions. The internet can anesthetize us in a similar way. The internet can tell us what we already know, but at the expense of dismissing what we have yet to discover.[150] In the same way, social media can imitate aspects of real relationships, but it lacks the intimacy of relationships with shared morals and beliefs.

I may go to church less and read more than when I was growing up, but it hasn't made me feel any smarter. In many ways, I feel less smart than ever before. Through years of reading and study, I may understand math and physics better than I used to, but that understanding has also revealed all that I don't know. The answers to old questions have led to

---

149    Farah Pandith, *How We Win: How Cutting-Edge Entrepreneurs, Political Visionaries, Enlightened Business Leaders, and Social Media Mavens Can Defeat the Extremist Threat* (New York: Custom House, 2019), p. 94.

150    Brian Grazer, *A Curious Mind: The Secret to a Bigger Life* (New Yorker: Simon & Schuster, 2015), loc. 2267, Kindle.

new as yet unanswered questions. Quantum mechanics explains many of the mysteries of the atom, but it doesn't explain why there is an atom. Gravitational fields may explain how objects and planets are pulled toward one another, but they don't explain why gravitational fields exist. Darwin's theory may have a lot more compelling evidence than the story of Noah, but evidence for Darwin's theory isn't unassailable and doesn't indisputably explain the origins of all creation. For that matter, all the studying that could ever be done will never answer why there is something instead of nothing. Science may leave fewer gaps, but the gaps still remain and are deeper than Copernicus, Galileo, or Newton could ever have imagined. Moreover, no matter how many and how deep the gaps, there is nothing else besides religion to fill them.

This is the crux of the hate between conservatives and liberals when it comes to religion. Psychologist Daniel Kahneman sums up the feeling well. "Our comforting conviction that the world makes sense rests on a secure foundation: our almost unlimited ability to ignore our ignorance."[151] The far-left liberal conviction that those who believe in some form of religion are uneducated, misinformed zealots reveals an underlying contempt for conservatives. It's the kind of snobbish pseudo intellectualism that ignores the complexity of life and all that remains mysterious. It drives the stake of hatred between religious Republicans and non-spiritual Democrats even further and pretends that the power offered by science and education is more important than the order offered by religion.

If science is about power and religion is about order, what gets lost is a pursuit of truth. Finding the truth was once the raison d'être of the

---

151    Ian Leslie, *Curious: The Desire to Know and Why Your Future Depends on It* (New York, Basic Books, 2014), p. 40.

media. Thus saying I no longer trust the media is the equivalent of saying I no longer know what is true. That is a tremendous problem and the subject of the next chapter.

## CHAPTER 6

★ ★ ★ ★ ★ ★ ★

# DIVIDED BY THE MEDIA

It is dangerous for old men to become nostalgic for the times when they were young men. Spending too much time looking in the rear view mirror of life, one runs the risk of letting regrets and disappointments of the past displace dreams and aspirations for the future. Life only moves forward, and the good old days never return. As I comb more gray hair, I fight the urge to think of days gone by as the guide for how things should be today. When that happens, I feel my mind closing off to the possibility of what might be, and I become a bit sad, as if the best times I will ever know have come and gone. Still, it is natural to be critical of the present in comparison to our past. George Orwell offered insight into that innate tendency when he wrote, "Every generation imagines itself to be more intelligent than the one that went before it, and wiser than the one that comes after it." With so much hatred being expressed toward one another today, I feel those nostalgic thoughts creeping in about how things used to be when I read or listen to the news.

Two generations ago, the options for learning about national news were limited. *CBS*, ABC, and *NBC* competed for the attention of Americans looking for news of the day during the dinner hour each evening. Walter Cronkite dominated the competition during his tenure at *CBS* in the 1960s and 1970s.[152] Cronkite oozed credibility. His soft, lyrical baritone voice came from a nearly expressionless face that gave the impression he was speaking the truth. Behind him on the *CBS* set during the telecast were other reporters manning telephones and typewriters. It was a very convincing scene that gave stories from the assassination of President Kennedy to the Watergate scandal an integrity absent from most media reports today. Cronkite's signature sign off at the end of each broadcast, "And that's the way it is . . ." followed by the day and date signaled a transition from the preceding half-hour of facts, to the fiction of *CBS* sitcoms and dramas that were to follow.

Those days of journalism are gone, and at the risk of being too nostalgic, I miss them. Cronkite had no catchy bumper music to lead in, no bespoke suits with Gucci ties, no over-the-top teasers for upcoming stories or tickers trawling along the bottom of the screen—just reporters and journalists doing what they were hired to do.

No matter the source, I have come to view journalism with such skepticism that I cannot read an article or watch a news program without focusing more on the bias than the story. The anti-capitalism, anti-Trump rhetoric of *MSNBC, CNN, BuzzFeed,* and the *HuffPost* (formally *The Huffington Post*) is matched by the right wing rants of *Fox News, Breitbart,* and the *New York Post*. Even traditionally mainstream media groups like *Reuters, Bloomberg,* and *AP* spend more column space interpreting the news rather than reporting it. It is one thing for

---

152   Albert Auster, "Columbia Broadcasting System," Museum of Broadcast Communications. Archived from the original on August 20, 2013.

journalists and editors to tell us which events they think we should know about, but their efforts to provoke thought become thinly veiled efforts to control thought when more effort is spent trying to convince us how we should feel about events than on the events themselves.

It is not a surprise that the media industry is struggling with a crisis of truth. In 82 percent of the countries around the world, less than half of the citizens trust the media.[153] In the United States, our political polarization is mirrored by the news sources we do and don't trust. *CNN* is trusted by 70 percent of self-described liberal Democrats but only 16 percent of conservative Republicans. Conversely, *Fox News* is trusted by 75 percent of conservative Republicans but only 12 percent of liberal Democrats.[154] In the United States, there is no longer a singular truth to be reported, only versions of the truth—versions that each of us choose based on our political ideology and taste for truthiness.

The absence of a singular truth undermines the media's credibility. The greatest long-term threat to journalism is the spread of suspicion and cynicism for the product they produce. It has become impossible to distinguish truths from half-truths. Newscasts and cable news programs offer brief reports of actual events followed by a lengthy panel discussion with other reporters, experts, and insiders telling us what the events mean and how those events should make us feel. Simultaneously, a few channels or clicks away, a different panel of reporters, experts, and insiders comes to a completely different conclusion as to what happened, what it means, and how we should feel. When the truth is malleable and trust in authority erodes, new knowledge fails to form

---

153    William Davies, *Nervous States: Democracy and the Decline of Reason* (New York: WW Norton, 2018), p. xiii.

154    John Gramlich, "Q&A: How Pew Research Center evaluated Americans trust in 30 news services," January 24, 2020. https://www.pewresearch.org/fact-tank/2020/01/24/qa-how-pew-research-center-evaluated-americans.

and progress grinds to a halt because there are no facts to debate and no reliable experts to offer perspective. Our search for truth becomes more of a quest for confirmation of our beliefs rather than a search for the undeniable facts—all of which is aided by technology that has allowed the creation of innumerable news sources.

Technology has always led to abundance. The loom created an abundance of clothes, the steam engine created an abundance of ship and train travel, the assembly line gave us an abundance of cars and washing machines. Now seamless, effortless communication has given us an abundance of news and commentary. Yet there is an important difference between prior technologies and those of today. While there is no limit to the types of clothes and cars people might want or the places they wish to travel, no matter how much news exists, it doesn't create more truth. More news only creates more anxiety and doubt about how elusive the truth has become.

There is so much media available today that an individual's news sources can become narrow and polarized. An abundance of news choices makes for fierce competition among media companies. Author James Gleick summarizes that competition nicely, "When information is cheap, attention becomes expensive."[155] It is hard to make an audience pay attention when they have nearly unlimited options. The best way to grab the audience's attention is to say and report things that they want to hear. A switch from reporting news to a broad audience to a focus on what the news means and how a carefully defined subgroup should feel about it has changed the newsroom in ways that would make Walter Cronkite wince.

---

155    James Gleick, quote, Goodreads. https://www.goodreads.com/quotes/393102-when-information-is-cheap-attention-becomes-expensive.

News today has less reporting and more persuasion. Reporting is about rational thought, but rational thought plays a very limited role in persuasion. Persuasion is about emotion. In an attempt to reach the most viewers of a similar political ideology, the media exchanges truth for audience empathy and engagement. As the audience gets bigger, the bullet points get shorter and the messages get simpler—a tendency that lends itself to 280 character tweets or fifteen-second *TikTok* videos. Members of the media assume the audience is willing to trade complex truth for the head-nodding security of being part of an audience subgroup that shares the same opinion about some oversimplified version of the truth. Presenting the truth takes time. The truth comes with context, subtlety, and consequences. The truth tasks the frontal and parietal lobes of the brain to engage in complex thought that considers the contradictions, inconsistencies, implications, and blind spots embedded in the truth.

Conversely, persuasion works through the primal, emotional portions of the brain in the temporal lobes and hypothalamus. Persuasion and influence tap into deeply seeded fears of losing control, power, money, or prestige. Persuasion and influence act quickly while understanding the truth requires time to think and reason.

It is often said by politicians and pundits that we are living in a post-truth world.[156] Post-truth is a modern word to describe an old problem. A post-truth world is one in which objective facts are less important in shaping public opinion than appeals to emotion or deeply held personal beliefs. It is the same type of world that existed for most of history prior to the scientific revolution and mass literacy—a time when "truth"

---

156    Jullian Birkinshaw, "The Post-Truth World - Why Have We Had Enough of Experts, *Forbes*, May 22, 2017. https://www.forbes.com/sites/lbsbusinessstrategyreview/2017/05/22/the-post-truth-world-why-have-we-had-enough-of-experts/?sh=5ed6d35354e6.

was limited to the words spoken by kings, priests, and oracles. A fascist society thrives in a post-truth world where the powerful oppress the powerless in the name of creating an improved, rejuvenated society. Fascist name-calling amplifies hatred amongst conservative Republicans and liberal Democrats, with one group calling out the other for such oppressive behavior.

In his book "Them," Nebraska senator Ben Sasse offers some insight into what drives news programming and contributes to a post-truth world. He reflects on his experience as a guest on cable news shows. Senator Sasse points out that there are only two kinds of stories on cable news. One type makes the people who love the channel love it more. The second makes the people who hate the channel hate it more. Both types of stories are designed to play on the emotions of their viewers rather than appeal to higher-order thinking.

Senator Sasse also notes that most national political reporters are very different from the people who read or watch their reports. Ninety-two percent of national political reporters have a college degree, only 7 percent are Republicans, and most live in either New York or Washington, D.C.[157] More importantly, national political reporters rarely meet with people who are different from them. Senator Sasse relays the compelling anecdote that when speaking with a reporter, he would first like to ask them a specific and revealing question. Here is the setup. The top three highest-selling vehicles in the United States are pickup trucks. Driving a pickup truck often suggests the owner comes from a working class culture and has the political leanings that usually go with it. For example, every person I know who raises cattle as I do in southwest Missouri drives a pickup. Being from a rural "flyover" state, Senator Sasse says he is curious whether the reporter about to interview

157    Sasse, *Them: Why We Hate Each Other*, 85.

him personally knows anyone that drives a pickup truck. The great likelihood is—probably not.[158]

Conservative political commentator and *New York Times* columnist David Brooks has written about this same inherent cultural media bias. "The big difference for those of us in the media is that the main story is not only where the decision makers are creating events. It's also and maybe more so in the eyes of those doing the perceiving."[159] When the media cannot be trusted because bias is so obvious and the reporter's perspective is so narrow, truth takes a back seat to advocacy, and journalism is more opinion than reporting. It is more "that's what we think" and the implication "that's what you should think" as opposed to "that's the way it is."

This is a situation that should be alarming to every American. A democratic government needs journalism, academia, and science to support it. Journalism is quickly failing at its crucial role and is contributing to a stark cultural change where the truth is elusive and trust vanishes. In fairness, not all the blame should fall on the media. From a different perspective, the media is simply giving its readers and viewers what they want. In the internet era, finding out what people like involves counting what they click on. Sadly, that often leads to quick-hit, audacious, often lewd content that is the equivalent of giving the audience a repetitive sugar rush. The ability to click and move quickly also makes the audience's attention span exceedingly short. Today, the average American attention span is eight seconds. For comparison, the

---

158    Sasse, *Them: Why We Hate Each Other*, 87.

159    David Brooks, "The Media is Broken", *New York Times*, December 26, 2019, https://www.nytimes.com/2019/12/26/opinion/media-politics.html.

attention span of a goldfish is nine seconds.[160] In the eighteenth century, symphony goers paid for an entire evening's worth of entertainment. In the twentieth century, the first vinyl records were able to store thirty minutes worth of music. That gave way to the single, which needed to be under 240 seconds.[161] Today, a *TikTok* video lasts fifteen seconds, and only 55 percent of Americans will spend more than fifteen seconds reading an online article.[162]

From a political perspective, a short attention span coupled with near infinite news and entertainment choices results in a less informed, more gullible voter. The uninformed American voter has been a lament of scholarly debate for generations. Such criticism has merit. Only one in three Americans can name the three branches of government.[163] While there is much more political information available in the internet era, there is also a lot more of everything else. From cat videos to recipes, competition for attention has never been greater. The rate-limiting step for a more informed voter is not the amount of information but the level of interest.

An abundance of media choices plays to our genetic predispositions. Despite having 99.9 percent of the same DNA, each of us is unique for two reasons. First, each of us has experiences and perspectives that are completely different from every other person. Second and more important for long-term behavior, each one of our brains makes a

---

160    Rohit Bhargava, *Non-Obvious: How to Think Different, Curate Ideas & Predict The Future* (Ideapress Publishing, 2015), loc. 1307, Kindle.

161    Derek Thompson, *Hit Makers: The Science of Popularity in an Age of Distraction* (New York: Penguin Random House, 2017), p. 13.

162    Sasse, *Them: Why We Hate Each Other*, 109.

163    Jared Meyer, *The Ignorant Voter*, June 27, 2016. https://www.forbes.com/sites/jaredmeyer/2016/06/27/american-voters-are-ignorant-but-not-stupid/.

unique set of connections based on those experiences and perspectives. Those neural connections shape who we are and the decisions we make. Consequently, each of us develops unique interests and tastes that compel us to seek out media that fits those interests and tastes.

As the cost of generating media content has been reduced over the past forty years, we have become a culture with few common media experiences. The most obvious example is the viewership of network television. Nielsen ratings have been used for the past seventy years to measure the audience size and composition of television programming. To have a Nielsen rating of twenty, one-fifth of all households with a television have to be watching the program. In 1979, twenty-six shows passed that threshold. In 1999, only two did: *ER* and *Friends*. By 2015, there were none.[164]

The lack of common cultural and media experiences opens the door to treating those that don't share our political ideology as somehow different from us. To be interested in politics, one has to cheer for a certain side and want a specific outcome. Just like the most informed sports fans are most committed to their teams, it is the most informed citizens that are most committed to their political affiliation and think voters on the other side are horrible. We argue online and share articles not to convince anyone of anything but rather to project a certain image of ourselves. It is the equivalent of joining a 1950s era club but without human contact. Increasingly, Americans look at their social, religious, and racial groups and see an alignment between them and a political party. That party identity keeps them grounded and connected to those in the group along with people to rally around. Once firmly implanted in a group and surrounded by like minds, introspection stops. Members

---

164    Derek Thompson, *Hit Makers: The Science of Popularity in an Age of Distraction* (New York: Penguin Random House, 2017), p. 242.

of the group may contend that they are open minded, but in the echo chamber of similar minds, hard questions are rarely asked. In the words of novelist Don Marquis, "If you make people think they're thinking, they'll love you; but if you really make them think, they'll hate you."[165]

The internet and social media have intensified our isolation and narrowed our perspective, but the internet and social media didn't create isolation. The late 1990s and early 2000s was a time when many people were already losing social connection with one another. Our obsessive use of social media, such as *Facebook, Twitter, Instagram,* and *Snapchat,* is an attempt to fill a void that was present and growing long before anyone had a smartphone.

There has always been moral fear about technology. We worry about the effects of social media today, but 2,400 years ago Socrates was worried about the Greek people learning to write because he feared no one would remember anything. Technology like social media is remarkably powerful and adept at stoking fear. Each day, one billion people log onto *Facebook.* One hundred and seventy million of those are from the United States and Canada.[166] The average American spends two-and-one-half hours per day on social media.[167] Forty-five percent of all Americans and 88 percent of all Americans under age thirty-five get their news from *Facebook.*[168] Social media is the place we let our family and friends know how great we're doing. In regular conversation, people spend about 30 percent of the time talking about themselves. Online it

---

165    Wikiquote, "Don Marquis." https://en.wikiquote.org/wiki/Don_Marquis.

166    Thompson, *Hit Makers,* 266.

167    "Average Time Daily Spent on Social Media," The Broadband Search. https://www.broadbandsearch.net/blog/average-daily-time-on-social-media.

168    Thompson, *Hit Makers,* 272.

is 80 percent.[169] Offline, one-on-one, we talk to people. Online, one-to-a-thousand, we talk about ourselves.

It's not that *Facebook* and the rest of social media are turning us into narcissists, but rather social media only reveals our narcissism. Privately, we want to be understood, but publicly we want to be interesting, even enviable. "Look at how great my life is! Look at my new car, new house, new puppy, new son, new granddaughter!" But reality doesn't match the hype. The more time you spend on *Facebook*, the more likely you are to experience negative physical health, negative mental health, and negative life satisfaction.[170] It also increases the amount of anxiety you feel as well as the number of diagnosed anxiety disorders. The top 25 percent of social media users aged nineteen to thirty-two report being twice as lonely as people who use it the least.[171]

Social media has squeezed the space between public and private language. It has become the simplest and most efficient way to embed new ideas and crush contrary opinions at a time when we need to listen the most. For example, in the last three months of the 2016 presidential campaign, the top twenty fake news stories gathered more shares, comments, and reactions than the top twenty stories from the major news outlets combined, including *The New York Times, The Washington Post,* and *The Huffington Post.* Seventy-five percent of people that see fake news headlines believe them to be true.[172]

---

169    Thompson, *Hit Makers,* 225.

170    Sasse, *Them: Why We Hate Each Other,* 196.

171    Brian Grazer, *Face to Face: The Art of Human Connection* (New York: Simon & Schuster, 2019), p. 6.

172    Jamie Susskind, *Future Politics: Living Together in a World Transformed by Tech* (Oxford, United Kingdom: Oxford University Press, 2018), p. 229.

When proof for and against approaches infinity, a cloud of suspicion hangs over every statement made. All news becomes fake news. Fake news is not new. It has been going on for centuries. For decades, people believed ads claiming that drinking Coca-Cola would lead to health and youthfulness when it was really increasing the risk of getting diabetes. The delicate balance of truth and fiction has been the soul of advertising for over one hundred years. "Our society finds truth too strong a medicine to ingest undiluted," observed journalist Ted Koppel.[173]

But social media has no need for such balance. Provocative social media is the only profitable social media. The simplest formula in politics for castigating the opposition is to quote a foolish attention seeker who says something crazy and then malign all people within the same opposition group. With that simple, effective strategy, social media has an unlimited opportunity to inflict harm but a minimal ability to heal. In order to forgive, one has to forget, and the internet never forgets. What recourse does someone have who is wrongly accused on social media?

Former Google chairman Eric Schmidt once said, "The Internet is the first thing that humanity has built that humanity doesn't understand. It is the largest experiment in anarchy we have ever had."[174] He was so right. The amount of insults and threats passing through social media each day is staggering. There is rarely a day that goes by without a story of someone taking offense to a comment or post on social media. The frequency is so great, it has become necessary to ramp up the adjectives for expressing outrage. Anger is the emotion used to describe how we feel when a restaurant doesn't have organic, vegan, gluten-free options.

---

173    "Not the Ten Suggestions," *The Christian Science Monitor*, August 6, 1987. https://www.csmonitor.com/1987/0806/ukop.html.

174    vinod, "10 most quotable quotes from Google's Eri Schmidt," Tech Monitor, April 2, 2014. https://techmonitor.ai/technology/10-most-notable-quotes-from-googles-eric-schmidt-4207960.

Apoplectic is the emotion to describe being put in *Facebook* jail for making inappropriate commentary. Aggravated is how we feel when there are too many skinny people at the gym. Seething is how we feel when so-called friends don't give a "Like" emoji to our most recent post. To take social media at face value would be to believe that America is in a perpetual state of shock and awe.

In the era of Walter Cronkite, insults were dealt with face-to-face. The risk of saying something offensive about someone was that the comment would somehow make its way back to that someone and result in an uncomfortable situation. Today, insults are dealt with keyboard to keyboard. Cyberbullying is the modern version of real bullying without the blood and bruises. But pounding the keyboard harder or tapping the angry-face emoji more times hasn't made us more emotionally resilient. Rather, it has left us with thinner skin, the topic of our next chapter.

# CHAPTER 7
★ ★ ★ ★ ★ ★ ★

# THIN SKIN

Karen and Chad (my names for them) seemed like nice people. The well-dressed couple was driving past our farm on an early spring day when they flagged me down in the tractor I was driving. If there is one constant for farmers and ranchers in southwest Missouri each spring it is this. There will be mud. Lots of mud. It is unavoidable. The gravelly and silt loam soils of southwest Missouri are uneven, rocky, and drain poorly. The melting snow and spring rains sit in tire tracks and cattle hoofprints on pastures and driveways like house guests who refuse to leave. Tractor tires pick up the mud and leave a sticky dark maroon trail wherever the tractor goes. On this particular spring day, the mud on my tractor tires was being left on the asphalt road outside our farm gate. As Karen and Chad pulled their attractive late-model sedan up alongside my tractor and rolled down their window, I opened the door and leaned out to hear what they had to say. Was it necessary, Karen wondered, for me to be driving the tractor today since I was tracking mud onto the road, which was getting their car dirty.

My friends tell me that I have an expressive face. Apparently, I communicate my emotions clearly without saying many words. Hence, I am a lousy poker player. Karen and Chad must have read my emotions quickly as they scanned my face waiting for a sign that I would yield to their wishes. No words came from my mouth, but they looked back at me indignantly, as though I was violating their right to drive on a clean road. They rolled up their window and sped away, as they no doubt shared a few choice words about my indifference to their "problem."

When problems become rare, we count more things as problems. For a dirty car to be a top-of-mind concern on a beautiful spring day, food, shelter, clothing, personal safety, and health must be cause for little concern. From the perspective of someone without those life essentials, we are fortunate to live at a time and in a place when a dirty car can even be counted as a problem. For the first time in history, infectious disease kills fewer people than old age, famine kills fewer people than obesity, and violence kills fewer people than accidents.[175] Violent crimes, including rape, assault, and robbery, are all on a downward trend and today are less than half their peak incidence from 1991.[176] Contrast our generations' situation with those of our great grandparents. In 1900, only half of those born that year made it to age forty. In that same year, the average American spent twice as much on funerals as medicine, only 2 percent took a vacation, and the only two recognized work holidays were Christmas and the 4th of July.[177] Today, the average American household spends $60,000 per year. Of that, 50 percent goes to

---

175   Yuval Noah Harari, *21 Lessons for the 21st Century* (New York: Penguin Random House, 2018), p. 16.

176   Bailey and Tupy, *Ten Global Trends*, 15.

177   Will, *The Conservative Sensibility*, 225.

household necessities like food, clothing, and rent/mortgage. In 1900, 80 percent of household spending went toward those necessities.[178]

From a population health, safety, and wealth perspective, there is no better time and no better place to be alive than right now in this country. But as the world around us has become better, we have become harsher critics of it. It is a quirk of human nature that discontent is highest when misery becomes bearable. When happiness is far away, the step in front of us holds the excitement of an unpredictable journey. But when happiness is within reach, the step in front of us bears the weight of all we have suffered along the way.

Treating happiness as a destination leads to our discontent. We don't become happy by living a peaceful and prosperous life. We become happy when our reality matches our expectations. The problem is that as our conditions improve, our expectations boom. No matter how much we have, it is our nature to want more. Revolutions aren't started by those who have continuously suffered from a lack of opportunity and power. Revolutions are started and supported by those who have had a taste of better things, who have seen or experienced a better way of life. Those who lack many things live in a state of constant longing, but those who are within an arm's length of the things they desire the most live in a state of perpetual anxiety that pushes them to upset the established order.[179]

One hundred years ago, future president Franklin Delano Roosevelt took on his newly diagnosed polio as many people of that era took on hardship—with a stiff upper lip. The pervasive attitude of the Depression-era generation was that anyone could become a victim

---

178   Bailey and Tupy, *Ten Global Trends*, 152.

179   Eric Hoffer, *The True Believer: Thoughts on the Nature of Mass Movements* (New York: Harper & Row, 1951), p. 29.

at any time. Injuries, accidents, and illness—even polio—were not special punishments for the unlucky. Such insults to the physical body were obstacles that had to be overcome. In comparison, today, of all working-age men who are not in the military or institutionalized, one in six, over twenty million men, are not working and are on some form of government subsistence.[180] That is not to say that it is undesirable for a society to take care of its mentally and physically ill or that funding a government safety net isn't good for a society's mental and physical health. Government subsistence does, however, suppress its citizens' fear. It suppresses an existential fear for physiologic needs and safety that, in turn, makes room in the conscious mind for less consequential concerns. Today someone can complain if there is mud on the road next to a farm or a Caucasian is serving customers food in a Jamaican restaurant. Victimhood has become something to praise rather than stoicism or heroism. No matter how slight the injustice may be, to be a victim is a victory, and those who claim to be oppressed are perceived as more pure or decent than everyone else. The thin skin of twenty-first century victimhood has obscured the difference between the suffering of those who are truly oppressed from the complaining of those who only want to be noticed.

It does not have to be this way. America was once a country of realists and pragmatists. As westward expansion advanced through the Great Plains in the nineteenth century, the harshness of the frontier made pioneers overcome real fears in order to survive. That resilience led to inventions, wealth, and power. Today, with greater control over our environment, we have become less prone to confront the harshness of our reality. Instead, we avoid it. We construct virtual fantasies to divert our attention and give us something to be excited about. We

---

180    Arthur C. Brooks, *The Conservative Heart: How to Build a Fairer, Happier and More Prosperous America (New York:* Harper Collins, 2015), p. 63.

attach personal meaning to innocuous actions and then exaggerate their significance to make us appear more victim-like. With each illusion, we became easier to deceive. We struggle to distinguish fact from fiction.[181]

The United States is not the first world power to struggle with the paradoxical thin skin that comes from power, wealth, and a life of relative luxury. The same thing happened in Rome, as once stoic and pragmatic citizens lost discipline and sought escape. The Romans became encumbered with petty political squabbles and ignored larger dangers on the outskirts of their empire as they eventually fell to the barbarians and, in defeat, found an escape from the harsh realities of keeping their empire intact.

While the Romans sought escape, Americans just want to feel good. From the seventeenth century to the middle of the twentieth century, accomplishment was the foundation on which self-esteem grew. American generations of that era were notoriously insecure and perceived that other nations were in a conspiracy to undervalue them. Without social designations, such as lord and commoner, one's status in a growing nation was a reflection of economic production. Every man and woman suffered from a longing to rise.[182] That insecurity remains the inherent Achilles' heel of capitalism and individualism in this country.

But in the latter half of the twentieth century, the order was reversed. Self-esteem became the precursor to achievement. Schools began to focus on building self-esteem rather than rewarding accomplishment. Self-esteem was separated from displaying self-esteem worthy behavior.[183] The

---

181 Robert Green and 50 Cent, *The 50th Law* (New York: G-Unit Books, 2009), p. 36.

182 Chua and Rubenfeld, *The Triple Package*, 85.

183 Chua and Rubenfeld, *The Triple Package*, 212.

self-esteem movement made Americans more satisfied with themselves, but it didn't make us better or solve any psychological, academic, or social problems. Then in the 1980s with the economy growing rapidly and our national insecurity fading, impulse control became passe and was replaced with a desire for instant gratification.[184] "If it feels good, do it!" was the moral imperative of the Woodstock generation.[185] The Woodstock generation raised Gen X and millennials with the same urgency for self-esteem and instant gratification. As a result, we have become a culture that loves accolades more than genuine achievement. We would rather feel the freedom of doing what we please than the weighty yoke of self-discipline. Trophies, ribbons, and certificates of achievement have become the point rather than the consequence, and worthy endeavors have been cheapened by an epidemic of ubiquitous specialness.

From a political perspective, a cultural shift away from achievement and self-discipline toward self-esteem and instant gratification has undermined our natural curiosities and drive for new knowledge. When every person's perspective is worthy of praise, expectations change. The internal doubt that asks "could I be wrong?" is replaced with the indignant thought of "how could I be wrong?" The apprehension of putting one's unproven ideas in the public domain is replaced by an untested certainty. "I must be right because I am special!" Public discourse grinds to a halt because no one can agree to facts that are now only a matter of opinion. The rigid conviction of certainty becomes more of a threat to the truth than outright lies.

---

184    Chua and Rubenfeld, *The Triple Package*, 214.

185    Richard Klein,"If It Feels Good, Don't Do It", *New York Times*, July 28, 1996. https://www.nytimes.com/1996/07/28/books/if-it-feels-good-don-t-do-it.html.

Those with untested certainty are fragile. Their skin becomes thin. Conversations that risk being offensive conclude quickly. They fail to differentiate between "I think you're wrong" and "I think you're stupid." Their minds equate "critical thinking" with "relentless criticism." Untested certainty fosters the creation of a victim class of people that are beyond criticism. To call out weaknesses or deficiencies of a member of the victim class is to be labeled a bully, using a position of power to belittle the powerless. It is easier and preferable to undermine a political opponent with accusations and character insults rather than articulate compelling arguments. The net effect is silence among groups that don't share the same certainties and an anger that builds up behind closed doors until it is unleashed as hate when the doors inevitably open.

When the bar for being offended is lowered so much that democratic debate has seized up, fear rules the day. Political conservatives withhold their true opinions out of fear—fear of being labeled as bigoted or insensitive. Fear is the oldest and strongest emotion known to humans. It is deeply ingrained in our nervous system and subconscious. Fear is basic and simple. But fears of being embarrassed or intimidated don't affect the brain the same way as the "fight or flight" fears of survival. As we have gained control over our environment and driven away basic survival fears, the emotional vacuum that remains is filled by fears about our status or whether people like us. We worry about our health, the future, our family, or aging well. Simple, intense survival fears give way to a generalized, low-level anxiety that grinds away at one's sense of well-being and vulnerability.

Politicians and political leaders use that low-level anxiety to persuade. When a leader plants a political flag defining a position of the group that is then spread by social media in a matter of seconds, pushing back against that position or planting a different flag takes great courage. For the renegades willing to do so, the public's perception of them and their status within the tribe is placed in jeopardy. Most of us are unwilling to put ourselves in such a position. It is simply easier to go along than to stand apart. Instead of pushing a different agenda and going against the grain, we rationalize why going along with the rest of the tribe makes sense. Author Robert Heinlein makes the same observation. "Man is not a rational animal; he is a rationalizing animal."[186] The smarter and more positively one views themselves, the harder the brain works to rationalize the position that keeps them within the status quo.[187] Being marginalized by the tribe may only be a psychological insult, but a brain primed with fear and generalized anxiety perceives a psychological insult the same as a physical threat.[188]

Harvard law professor Lawrence Lessig makes an interesting observation about the moment we live in. "A time is marked not so much by ideas that are argued about as by ideas that are taken for granted."[189] In a slightly different way, Lessig points to the same quirk of human nature that we started with in this chapter. Our relative prosperity blinds us to the suffering of the generations that came before us. We live in the most secure, prosperous time in history. Technologies are advancing, old business models are dissolving, and every industry is wide open for innovation. It is a time of rapid, sweeping change. But with change comes significant challenges. The economy has undeniable vulnerabilities and is in need of reinvention. The lifespan of the average American has

---

186     Robert Heinlein, Conversational Leadership. https://conversational-leadership.net/quotation/quote-man-is-not-a-rational-animal/.

187     Alan Jacobs, *How To Think: A Guide for the Perplexed* (New York: Penguin Random House, 2017), p. 58.

188     Aaron T. Beck, *Prisoners of Hate: The Cognitive Basis of Anger, Hostility, and Violence* (New York: Harper Collins, 2010), p. 107.

189     Lawrence Lessig, "The Future of Ideas", *New York Times*, January 6, 2002. https://www.nytimes.com/2002/01/06/books/chapters/the-future-of-ideas.html.

decreased for the first time in over one hundred years, primarily due to drug and alcohol abuse and suicide amongst younger Americans.[190] Real wages for Americans with a high school diploma or less continue to decline.[191] There are far too many incidents of police brutality as we continue to struggle with issues of race, inequality, and polarization. But one of the best questions for those who believe our society is racist, sexist, homophobic, or monstrous is "compared to what?" What country in what era has shown the world how to deal with these issues? What has worked in the past or what system should we switch to that will work better than what we are already doing? Moreover, if the United States is so bad, why are so many people trying to immigrate here by any means necessary? In comparison, how many people are trying to immigrate to China, Russia, Japan, Germany, or any other U.S. rival?

The era of thin skin has to end. We cannot foster a culture that shuts out those whose ideas make us uncomfortable, those who think differently, those who disagree with us, or even those who hold different values. We cannot continue to attach personal meaning to innocuous actions and then exaggerate their significance. After behaving like a bully, one cannot find shelter from the resulting pushback by claiming they are the ones being bullied. No government will ever legislate away all hardship or outlaw evil people. No government could ever deliver on a theoretical right to live without suffering, and even if such a right existed, the consequences would be devastating. Author James Baldwin says it more

---

190    Laurel Wamsley, "American Life Expectancy Dropped on Full Year in 1st Half of 2020," NPR.org, February 18, 2021. https://www.npr.org/2021/02/18/968791431/american-life-expectancy-dropped-by-a-full-year.

191    Congressional Research Service, *Real Wage Trends, 1979 to 2019* (report R45090), December 28, 2020. https://fas.org/sgp/crs/misc/R45090.pdf.

colorfully, "People who cannot suffer cannot grow up, and can never discover who they are."[192]

Our attempt to avoid suffering is contributing to our anxiety. Conversations that are avoided leave important issues unsolved. Decisions that are postponed delay progress. Dealing with fear passively to avoid suffering is disempowering. It makes us victims in our own country. Learning to deal with fear more actively doesn't just happen. No one is born fearless, nor does anyone simply stop being fearful. Courage is not the absence of fear but rather taking action in spite of fear. It takes courage to have difficult conversations and make hard decisions. People who overcome their fears to have difficult conversations and make hard decisions come from all walks of life and cultures—from Socrates to Abraham Lincoln, Napoleon, Frederick Douglas, FDR, Rosa Parks, and Martin Luther King. Each of these courageous people acknowledged having the same fears we all have of standing apart from custom and conventional wisdom. None of them knew how history would judge their actions or if they would be remembered at all. What they did have was a sense of urgency. In Rosa Parks' own words, "I have learned over the years that when one's mind is made up, this diminishes fear; knowing what must be done does away with fear."[193]

If the conversations we need to have the most fail to happen because we fear offending or being offended, our time as a world power will come to a close. Powerful countries and powerful people display courage. They display the type of courage that does not seek to offend but does seek to challenge. Contrary to the prevailing opinion, most powerful

---

192    "James Baldwin, The Fire Next Door." http://crab.rutgers.edu/~glasker/BALDWINCR.htm.

193    Peter Economy, "17 Empowering Quotes From Strong Women," Inc., May 10, 2018. https://www.inc.com/peter-economy/17-empowering-quotes-from-strong-women.html.

people do not have thick skin. Instead, they tend to have skin that is sensitive to what others say about them. But unlike the thin skin of those with untested certainty, powerful people can respond to negativity by becoming better. They respond to raised voices by making a better argument. They respond to obstacles by finding a way through, over, or around. They respond to challenges, knowing their journey will include sacrifice and suffering. This has been the path of progress for millennia. The generations alive at this moment have unique challenges, but so has every generation that has come before us. We are no different, and we are not special. It is time for us to raise the level of our conversation. It is time to call out what we fear and act in spite of those fears. It is time for us to rebuild trust in our institutions and one another. That is the subject of our next chapter.

# CHAPTER 8
★ ★ ★ ★ ★ ★ ★

# DISTRUST IN SCIENCE

In 2006, former vice president Al Gore released a documentary film about climate change called An Inconvenient Truth. The film is a slideshow presentation with detailed graphs, flow charts, and stark photographs of the earth taken from space. After making the case that climate change is a result of man's use of fossil fuels, Gore states that climate change is not a political issue but rather a moral issue. The implication is that decent people with good morals would join him in the fight against climate change. He then veers into predictions based on the data just presented. Gore claims that if greenhouse gas emissions are not cut in ten years, climate change will reach a point of no return and that sea levels could rise by 20 feet, creating 100 million refugees. The documentary won two Academy Awards, including one for Best Documentary Feature.[194] Thirteen years later, three years past Gore's predicted point of no return

---

194    Wikipedia, "An Inconvenient Truth," modified September 10, 2021. https://en.wikipedia.org/wiki/An_Inconvenient_Truth.

date, fellow Democrat and New York representative Alexandria Ocasio-Cortez doubled down on climate change predictions claiming "the world is going to end in twelve years if we don't address climate change."[195]

The moxy that it takes to make such dire predictions is admirable. People say they want to hear the truth, but every politician knows that when talking about the future, the people want to hear optimism from them. Rising sea levels, 100 million refugees, and a fiery end to the world don't sound optimistic. But in this instance, Gore and Ocasio-Cortez don't want to be seen as politicians. Rather, they are trying to act like reliable experts worthy of our trust, and pessimistic experts always sound smarter than optimistic ones. Nineteenth-century economist and philosopher John Stuart Mill had the same perception, "I have observed that it is not the man who hopes when others despair, but the man who despairs when others hope, who is admired by a large class of persons as a sage."[196]

In their defense, what Gore and Ocasio-Cortez are doing is what we all do when our minds are given a chance to rest. We think about the future. Our brains are non-stop prediction machines. At rest, our mind spends three times more thinking about the future than the past. Even thoughts about the past are about how bygone events might affect our future.[197] We want to be able to see around the corner to catch a glimpse

---

195    William Cummings, "The world is going to end in 12 years if we don't address climate change, Ocasio-Cortez says," *USA Today*, January 22, 2019. https://www.usatoday.com/story/news/politics/onpolitics/2019/01/22/ocasio-cortez-climate-change-alarm/2642481002/.

196    Gautam Baid, *The Joys of Compounding: The Passionate Pursuit of Lifelong Learning* (New York, Columbia University Press, 2020), p. 271.

197    Steven Johnson, *Farsighted: How We Make the Decisions That Matter the Most* (New York: Riverhead Books, 2018), p. 80.

of the future and those in a position of power who say they can draw our attention.

The problem with such bold predictions coming from political leaders in the know is that they make a very complex issue sound too simple. The earth's climate is an enormously complex interplay between wind, ocean currents, atmospheric circulation, the tilt of the earth's axis, the concentration of plant and animal life, solar radiation, and greenhouse gases, just to name a few. Both Gore and Ocasio-Cortez would have us believe that on the topic of climate change they have suspended themselves from the usual persuasive tactics that politicians use on their constituents. When it comes to climate, they are relying on the objectivity of science, and science, in this case, agrees with them. They insist they have managed to understand the complexity of climate science, distilled it down to slideshow and audio sound-bite simplicity, and are able to predict our doomsday down to the year.[198] If that were true, their predictions would stand in contrast to most predictions made by geological experts over the past century.

In 1914, the U.S. Bureau of Mines claimed that all U.S. oil reserves would be exhausted by 1924. In 1939, the U.S. Department of the Interior reported that the entire world's oil reserves would be exhausted by 1953. In 1970, it was widely accepted that the world's total oil reserve was 612 billion barrels, and in 1977, President Carter told Americans those reserves would be used up by 1990. Yet somehow, by 2006, 767 billion barrels had been pumped and proven reserves now numbered 1.2 trillion barrels.[199] In 1968, Stanford professor and MacArthur Genius

---

198    Alison N. P. Stevens, "Factors Affecting Climate Change," *Nature Education Knowledge* 3, no. 10 (2011), p. 18. https://www.nature.com/scitable/knowledge/library/factors-affecting-global-climate-17079163/.

199    Will, *The Conservative Sensibility*, 259.

Award winner Paul Ehrlich predicted that the race for humanity was over, hundreds of millions of people in India and Pakistan were going to die from starvation, and there was nothing anyone could do about it. In 1972, computer models at MIT affirmed that prediction and forecast the end of the world to be in the early twenty-first century due to nonrenewable resource depletion and population growth. Despite those dire predictions from respected experts, India and Pakistan doubled their wheat production, India became a net exporter of food, and the world increased its population by 210 percent.[200] In the 1960s, government experts said the Philippines would be the world's next big economy.[201] In the 1970s, the Federal Reserve reported that high inflation would be a permanent part of American culture.[202] In the 1980s, nearly every news outlet in existence was convinced that Japan would dominate the world economy during our lifetime due to their manufacturing prowess and management practices.[203] In the 1990s, foreign policy experts were certain that lowering the iron curtain would unleash Soviet and Eastern European capabilities, making them the next center of economic growth in the world.[204] Of course, none of these predictions have come true. Moreover, these wrong predictions highlight the inherent flaw of blindly believing in science. Science is a process of prediction, theory, testing, and proving. Experiments are done and conclusions are made. Subsequently, those conclusions are subject to further testing and validation. Sometimes those conclusions hold up; often they don't. In

---

200    Donald Sull, *The Upside of Turbulence: Seizing Opportunity in an Uncertain World* (New York: Harper Collins, 2009), loc. 329, Kindle.

201    Ruchir Sharma, *The Rise and Fall of Nations: Forces of Change in the Post-Crisis World* (New York: W. W. Norton, 2016), p. 6.

202    Robert S. Kaplan, *What You Really Need to Lead: The Power of Thinking and Acting Like an Owner* (Boston, MA: Harvard Business Review Press, 2015), p. 154.

203    Kaplan, *What You Really Need to Lead*, 154.

204    Sharma, *The Rise and Fall of Nations*, 7.

early 2021, virus experts reported in reputable journals that Covid-19 was not man-made but rather had a "natural origin." One month later, those same experts were not so sure.[205]

One of the long-term consequences of bold, wrong predictions by politicians and scientists is that they undermine trust in the people who make them and by association, government, science, and expertise. Yet, the more complex the world around us becomes, the more analysis and predictions are put forth by a growing number of ever more specialized scientists and experts to explain what is happening and what is yet to come. For example, in medicine, the general practitioner is a relic of the twentieth century. Medicine has been divided into pediatrics, obstetrics, surgery, radiology, and more than 135 other specialties and subspecialties that focus physicians on understanding, diagnosing, and treating specific illnesses.[206] When Senator Ted Kennedy underwent surgery to resect a malignant brain tumor, experts such as neuro-oncologists and neurosurgeons specializing in malignant gliomas weighed in on his treatments and prognosis.[207] No one was interested in what his general practitioner had to say about that topic. Similarly, engineering has gone from four major branches—chemical, electrical, mechanical, and civil—to over forty different degrees and hundreds of subcategories to understand our physical world and find practical solutions to technical

---

205    "Fact Check: How the Wuhan lab-leak theory for pandemic origin suddenly became credible," *The Seattle Times*, May 25, 2021. https://www.seattletimes.com/nation-world/fact-check-how-the-wuhan-lab-leak-theory-for-pandemic-origin-suddenly-became-credible/.

206    "Specialty Profiles," Careers in Medicine, AAMC website. https://www.aamc.org/cim/explore-options/specialty-profiles#.

207    Miranda Hitti, "Sen. Ted Kennedy out of Brain Surgery," WebMD, June 2, 2008. https://www.webmd.com/cancer/brain-cancer/news/20080602/sen-ted-kennedy-to-get-brain-surgery.

problems.[208] When earthquakes began to happen in Texas, Oklahoma, and other fracking states, the news was full of expert opinions from seismologists, petroleum engineers, and groundwater hydrogeologists to explain what was happening and what to expect.[209] These may be the only specialists in the world with enough knowledge about the interaction between rock, water, and preexisting faults to understand what was happening two miles underground.

An exponential rise in the amount of data and information generated by specialization has resulted in even more narrow areas of expertise. But an abundance of information has come with the unwanted baggage of mistrust. Between the years 1996 and 2011, twenty-five million academic papers were published by fifteen million scientists from around the world. When academics examined the validity of those papers, 85 percent were determined to be worthless. Many of the most influential studies failed to be replicated. The primary finding was that the authors made exaggerated claims about the validity of their results.[210]

Exaggerated findings are not the only misleading consequence of greater specialization and more data. An abundance of scientists combined with the low cost of producing and distributing information has resulted in a growing number of scientific journals. Best estimates indicate that there are now over thirty thousand scientific journals publishing more than

---

208    "40 Different Types of Engineering Degrees," Types of Engineering Degrees. https://typesofengineeringdegrees.org.

209    Nathan Bernier, "Earthquake in South Texas: Fracking Fluid at Fault?" KUT, Austin's NPR, October 20, 2011. https://www.kut.org/energy-environment/2011-10-20/earthquake-in-south-texas-fracking-fluid-at-fault.

210    Edward Tenner, *The Efficiency Paradox: What Big Data Can't Do* (New York: Penguin Random House, 2018) p. 172.

two million articles annually.[211] Many of the new ones are open-source journals that avoid the rigorous peer-review standards used to validate the authors' results. But scientific journals without peer review are hard to distinguish from those with peer review.

Even with peer review, subject matter has become so specialized that only a handful of people can understand the research on a particular subject. Authors and reviewers often trade places in a circle of mutual admiration and protection. In extreme cases, a cabal of scientists representing one perspective keep out minority or unorthodox views. In this way, the scientific establishment has paralleled behavior by the mainstream media to monopolize information and claim absolute authority.[212] Distinguishing between real and fake science is just as hard as it is to distinguish between real and fake news, making bumper stickers claiming, "I Believe in Science" about as convincing as ones requesting fellow motorists to, "Follow Me to Hogwarts".

Public distrust is compounded when science and politics mix. Such mixing is inevitable since much of the money for science comes from political systems. Moreover, scientists, like everyone else, have political opinions that find their way into science. But when science and politics bleed together, the definition of an expert becomes a credentialed person who is in agreement with the desired outcome. In the internet era, those people are only a few clicks away. Recently, when emails of leading climatologists were hacked, revealing that they had less confidence in the methods of assessing the earth's historic temperatures than previously reported (historic temperature data is based on tree rings, polar ice core

---

211    Philip G. Altbach and Hans de Wit, "Too much academic research is being published," September 7, 2018. https://www.universityworldnews.com/post. php?story=20180905095203579.

212    Martin Gurri, *The Revolt of the Public and the Crisis of Authority in the New Millennium* (San Francisco, CA: Stripe Press), p. 180.

samples, and fossilized single-cell organisms[213]), the response of the woke scientific community was not for more research to sort out the uncertainty but to circle the wagons and call for less dissension.[214] That is how political movements and religions work, not science.

The dilemma created for scientists outside the woke community is choosing between displaying a very unscientific passion for their particular position or to portray a demeanor of cold rationality that can seem arrogant, distant, and unrelatable. Much of the time, the wisest thing to do is nothing, which is less contentious, but when contrarian views disappear, it reinforces a public perception that scientists are colluding with each other to further their own interests.

When scientists do speak up, personal attacks are just as effective as discrediting their research. Mobile phones and social media that capture the private whims and foibles of scientists or other experts are a gift to those who wish to discredit them. The vivid details dismantle the capacity of the public to place a divide between an expert's personal life and public interest. As the divide between public and private life disintegrates, the disinterested perspective of the scientist also deteriorates. The virtual crowd that gathers around the issue du jour generates a swarm of zealots who may or may not understand the issue but clearly have strong feelings. In these online viral moments, there is no representation or debate, just mobilization based around the crowd's emotional intensity. Harvard linguist Steven Pinker was the subject of such an attack in 2020 when a group of 600 people wrote an open letter to the Linguistic Society of America demanding his removal as a

---

213    Caitlin Keating-Bitonti and Lucy Change, "Here's How Scientists Reconstruct Earth's Past Climates," *Smithsonian Magazine*, March 23, 2018. https://www.smithsonianmag.com/blogs/national-museum-of-natural-history/2018/03/23/heres-how-scientists-reconstruct-earths-past-climates/.

214    Gurri, *The Revolt of the Public*, 184.

distinguished fellow of that organization. The group based its demand on six incidents when Pinker sent out tweets citing studies and op-eds supporting his argument that racism in the United States is weakening and that violence and injustice is on the decline. After Pinker made a thorough rebuttal of each accusation, he noted the ferocity of the group's shared emotion to get him canceled. He lamented the tactic of "trolling through tweets and through statements seeking to find evidence—however tortured—that there are signs of prejudice behind them."[215]

Principled, informed arguments are a sign of intellectual health and vitality in a democracy, but we live in an age when misinformation pushes aside those types of arguments. Thus, it is no surprise that trust is decreasing in scientists and experts and increasing in "people like me." For the first time in recorded history, trust is simultaneously decreasing not just in science but also business, media, and the government.[216] It is more compelling to believe someone we know, who shares similar beliefs or has had similar experiences, than it is to believe an expert that may be credentialed but lacks familiarity. People on the left believe science is a tool of big business that wants to give us genetically modified everything. Those on the right believe that science is a tool the government uses to create a narrative around climate change and other leftist causes. The distrust on both sides isn't misplaced. Business does pay for a substantial part of scientific research, and the most important factor in research is garnering government favor, which is given out conditionally based on power and political advantage.[217]

---

215    Ronald Bailey, "Steven Pinker Beats Cancel Culture Attack," Reason, July 10, 2020. https://reason.com/2020/07/10/steven-pinker-beats-cancel-culture-attack/.

216    Jeremy Heimans and Henry Timms, *New Power: How Power Works in Our Hyperconnected World—and How to Make It Work for You* (New York: Penguin Random House, 2018), p. 24.

217    Gurri, *The Revolt of the Public*, 186.

Those beliefs, coming from different political angles, lead to the same collective sense that science and expertise are taking our autonomy. To reject expert advice is to take back some of that autonomy. But taking a contrarian view of expertise is not always helpful and can take us down a specious path. Reading articles off the internet is not the same as understanding an issue. Comprehension is not the same as analysis. Providing expertise is not a parlor game played with factoids. Being an expert takes hard work. We all overestimate ourselves, but the less competent do it more often. Less competent people use the word "certain" a lot. Certainty is a belief in your beliefs. Certainty is a barricade. It is an illusion that makes us feel smart and in control. Unlike the desire to learn that defines curiosity, once we are certain, we avoid any information that threatens our certitude. Certainty is the low road past hard problems and tough questions. Certainty is cowardice—a flight from the possibility that we might be wrong. Certainty is compounded by social media where fact and fiction are nearly indistinguishable. "The internet is not just a magnet for the curious, it is also a sinkhole for the gullible," says *The New York Times* journalist Frank Bruni.[218]

As an example, Google the word "evolution" and see what rabbit holes one could go down. After the first few pages linking to thoughtful analysis from Wikipedia, *National Geographic*, and scientific journals, comes page after page of links to blogs and opinion pieces that are just bizarre. If those pieces were taken at face value, the only possible conclusion would be that evolution is a Satanist plot rather than one of the most insightful scientific theories of all time. At a moment when everyone can make their opinion available for the online world to read, not all views are worthy of consideration if they are too fantastic or inane. Yet

---

218   Tom Nichols, *The Death of Expertise: The Campaign against Established Knowledge and Why It Matters* (New York: Oxford University Press, 2017), loc. 1659, Kindle.

this disconnect between fact and fiction is where the seeds of hatred lie. With science and expertise having been undermined by decades of wild predictions and information that is either unreliable or untrustable, belief becomes fact. If you believe the world will end in twelve years due to climate change—good enough. But if you don't believe it, then what? According to Al Gore, your disbelief is not a science issue but rather a moral one. Good people with good morals should believe the right things. They believe what other good people believe. Like those who are devout in their religion, they don't question. What happens next is a clash of certainties. One side is certain that the other is some combination of immoral, stupid, arrogant, or contemptuous. What is created is another us and them, another reason to distrust, and another reason to hate.

Science has created this divide, but the government has partnered with science to do so. The interplay between science and the government makes it hard to determine where one ends and the other begins and compounds the feeling of false expertise. The role the government plays in furthering that divide is the subject of the next chapter.

# CHAPTER 9

★ ★ ★ ★ ★ ★ ★ ★

# GOVERNMENT, POWER, AND HATE

Neurosurgery residency is a long slog. It's seven years of late nights and early mornings following eight years of medical school and undergraduate studies. Thousands of hours are spent learning how to manage and perform surgery on patients with brain and spine problems. Because neurosurgery is a specialty with only a few thousand members, it relies on a small but prolific group of academic neurosurgeons who work at medical schools. They teach residents and perform most of the research that helps move the specialty forward. To encourage residents to consider an academic career, two years of each neurosurgery residency are set aside for residents' own research. The two years are a wonderful time to slow down a bit, think deeply about a particular area of interest, and decide if an academic career is the right path. With a background in medicine and law, I was able to spend one of my research years doing a healthcare policy fellowship on Capitol Hill. As part of that fellowship,

I worked as a legislative aide for a U.S. senator researching healthcare issues and meeting with all types of lobbyists and consultants who wanted some type of help from the government. Most commonly, there were funding requests for research in a particular area or coverage of a new medical device or technology. It was an eye-opening experience.

One of the first things that stood out to me was how young most of the staff were who worked on Capitol Hill. Many are bright, ambitious people fresh out of college who come to Washington, D.C., hoping to make a difference. They make little money and live in tiny apartments but get to work on really interesting problems and rub elbows with many of their political heroes. There is a robust turnover of these young staffers, as they either lose their idealism or gain the experience they were looking for and turn their contacts and experiences into better paying gigs in the private sector. The same turnover occurs with their bosses, the elected officials.

Politicians that either leave or are voted out of Congress often become consultants and lobbyists for all types of companies and law firms. With their ability to get power players to answer the phone, they can be very helpful in obtaining government funding or advising staff on regulations that might benefit their clients. Access is a valuable asset to sell in Washington, D.C.

There were two other impressions that I took away from my experiences on Capitol Hill. The first was that, most of the time, an elected official knows very little about the subject matter before them. The best politicians are able to relate to a wide variety of people on a dizzying array of issues. But the price of knowing a little about many things is not knowing a lot about one thing. As such, senators and representatives rely on their young staffers to have background meetings with relevant companies, advocacy groups, and lobbyists to help draft legislation.

The second impression I left with was that the hearing rooms in the congressional office buildings and U.S. Capitol are political theaters where actors and actresses come to do their best work. Witnesses coming to testify in front of Congress prepare a few minutes of legally defensible remarks. After that, they nervously wait and wipe small beads of sweat from their foreheads while answering questions from the elected officials before them who sit in high-backed leather chairs on an elevated platform. Most of the time, the witnesses are not the best actors and actresses in the room. They struggle with words and lean back awkwardly to hear the advice of the lawyers sitting behind them before responding to questions. They do their best but typically come across as scared and apprehensive. The power differential between the witnesses and their interrogators is deliberate and effective.

Politicians tend to be much better actors and actresses. They have had time to hone their craft with a thousand stump speeches and fundraisers. Cameras and reporters show up for the most contentious hearings, which are good times for them to score points with their constituents. In comparison to the scared witnesses in front of them, senators and representatives know what questions they are going to ask and the outcome they want to see. Staffers sit behind them with supporting documents and subject matter knowledge if they need it. Senators and representatives also have the good fortune of knowing which people in the room are for and against them. In many cases, the outcome is already known. The hearing merely serves as a place to stage the theatrics that will communicate the messages they want their colleagues and constituents to remember.

Recently, I watched congressional hearings with technology CEOs.[219] As always, it was good theater, if you are into that sort of thing. In this instance, however, the roles of witnesses and interrogator appeared to be reversed, with senators and representatives looking more nervous than the CEO witnesses before them. Politicians feigned anger at the CEOs for breaches of privacy or unauthorized regulation of free speech knowing that they understood little and could do even less without running afoul of the public's desire for an open internet and free social media. Watching the politicians fumble with the science and technology vocabulary made the government look weak and ineffective compared to the calm and assured CEOs. Government weakness relative to technology's power is a trend, accelerated by a culture and economy becoming frightfully complex, which undermines public trust. This weakness makes an impression that the world has become too complex for the government to manage, let alone lead.

The aims of our government have changed over the past fifty years. The goal of government for the greatest generation (those born between 1900 and 1930) was to destroy the present and create a better future. Energy, infrastructure, space travel, and medicine were new frontiers, with opportunities for the government to prove itself. Today, particularly as the United States withdraws from international affairs and conflicts, our government just wants people to be happy—especially with it. If a group is victimized, disabled, troubled, below average, offended, or uncomfortable, it is the perceived role of the government to right that wrong and to be recognized for trying. There are no boundaries for what is on the table, but there are no epic consequences either. The chief ambition is to feel the public's pain, give money to a cause, or take

---

219    A recap can be seen in this video: The Late Show with Stephen Colbert, "Zuck Explains Facebook to Congress," YouTube video, 3.20. April 12, 2018. https://www.youtube.com/watch?v=Zo5Qlu9Xu3E.

an enlightened position. Our elected officials only ask that we let them finish their terms, make a donation, and help get them reelected.[220]

Gone are the days when the government tackled big problems like nuclear power, interstate highways, and lunar exploration. It now behaves like a big insurance company between Medicare, Social Security, and other entitlement programs. The government doesn't want to do anything with the money it collects from taxation; it just throws money at its biggest problems—the ones that don't respond to bullets.

Despite its shortcomings, government is still the best tool mankind has come up with to preserve order within the borders of its rule. Government offers stability over time so that plans can be made and put into action. The two oldest and most relied-upon functions of government are to monopolize force in order to maintain internal peace and to redistribute wealth. To the disengaged observer, our government's capacity to do the former is suspect. In the summer of 2020, protestors overwhelmed local security forcing mayors in Portland, Seattle, Chicago, Pittsburgh, and St. Louis to abandon their homes.[221] Shockingly, this was occurring while liberals continued to call for the defunding of police departments.[222] Defunding efforts were successful in metropolitan cities like Minneapolis, Baltimore, Philadelphia, Portland,

---

220   Gurri, *The Revolt of the Public*, 245.

221   Katie Shepherd, As Protestors Arrive at Their Doorsteps, Democratic Mayors in Portland, St. Louis Abandon Their Homes, *The Washington Post*, September 3, 2020. https://www.washingtonpost.com/nation/2020/09/03/mayors-portland-st-louis-protests/.

222   Maya King, "How 'Defund the Police' went from moonshot to mainstream," Politico, June 17, 2020. https://www.politico.com/news/2020/06/17/defund-police-mainstream-324816.

and San Francisco.[223] During the chaos of the Minneapolis protest, in what has to be one of the most ludicrous responses by an elected public official in U.S. history, city council president Lisa Bender was asked by a *CNN* reporter who the public should call in the middle of the night if their home is broken into and the police force has been dismantled. She replied, "I know that (question) comes from a place of privilege, for those of us for whom the system is working."[224]

If Ms. Bender or anyone else is wondering what might happen when the government abdicates its role of monopolizing force to maintain internal peace, lessons from the former Soviet Union might be instructive. In the early 1990s after the fall of the iron curtain, every government run service, including the police, was defunded. State assets were privatized, businesses were forced to pay for protection, and Russian gangsters became the monopolizing force within the country.[225] Ms. Bender should take note. The vacuum left by the absence of law and order will always be filled by someone, and that someone may not always have the public's best interest in mind.

As U.S. culture becomes more complex, the government struggles to lead effectively. Governments, particularly democracies, are typically good at maintaining the status quo but dismally bad at change because their nature is a slow, grinding dance of compromise. A government is

---

223    Jemima McEvoy, "At Least 13 Cities Are Defunding Police Departments," *Forbes,* August 13, 2020. https://www.forbes.com/sites/jemimamcevoy/2020/08/13/at-least-13-cities-are-defunding-their-police-departments/?sh=5cddeebe29e3,

224    Tristan Justice, "*CNN* Guest: Not Wanting to Be Raped and Robbed Is White Privilege," The Federalist, June 8, 2020. https://thefederalist.com/2020/06/08/*CNN*-guest-not-wanting-to-be-raped-and-robbed-is-white-privilege/.

225    Mark Galeotti, "Gangster's paradise: how organized crime took over Russia," *The Guardian*, March 23, 2018. https://www.theguardian.com/news/2018/mar/23/how-organised-crime-took-over-russia-vory-super-mafia.

a reflection of the people who create it and the citizens who consent to its laws and regulations. At its worst, government is a measure of what its citizens are willing to tolerate. In that way, "Every nation has the government it deserves," as French philosopher Joseph de Maistre once said.[226] As our nation's social pyramid becomes steeper, those closer to the base than the apex feel more at the mercy of governing elites that do not appear to be elite of character.

There is perhaps no better example of the hate that people have for the government than the Occupy Wall Street movement in 2011. The protestors claimed their hatred of a predatory economy, a corrupt government, and a society ruled by money. The Occupy Wall Street movement was about repudiation. Protestors had no demands but were full of accusations. Such repudiation and rebellion is often full of complaints but offers nothing in the way of solutions. Oddly, the response of then President Obama to Occupy Wall Street was to point out the sinful nature of the United States and the blunt machinery of government.[227] His comment revealed the growing weakness of the government. If the highest ranking U.S. official has no faith in the government to solve a big problem, then the distrust of everyone else seems justified.

The Occupy Wall Street movement pointed out the old power structure of government that Obama felt powerless to fix. Old power is like a financial currency. Those who have it want to keep it, grow it, and use it wisely for their own betterment. It is closed, inaccessible to those that don't have it, and hierarchical. What Occupy Wall Street and a new generation of leaders want is new power. New power is like an electrical

---

226    John Brooks, *Business Adventures: Twelve Classic Tale from the world of Wall Street* (New York: Integrated Media, 2014), p. 111.

227    Gurri, *The Revolt of the Public*, 152.

current. It can be both made and accessed by many. The goal of new power is not to hoard it but to channel it to those that can best put it to use.

Old power is enabled by what people or organizations exclusively know, own, or control. When old power loses its exclusivity and what it has becomes public, its power is lost. In contrast, new power is enabled by the activity of the crowd. The more people share knowledge, ownership, and control, the more power is generated. Old power models ask that we comply or consume. New power models ask that we share and create. Old power is driven by leaders. New power is driven by peers.[228]

For those with old power, people with new power are threatening. Those with old power have paid their dues. They need the status quo to endure for their old power to be valuable. New power people don't want what old power offers. New power is less about creating and managing organizations and more about temporary, less constraining affiliations.[229]

The difference between old and new power can be seen in traditional media versus social media. Traditional media thrived on exclusive stories, interviews, and editorial opinion. In contrast, social media is about sharing. *Facebook*, *Twitter*, Pinterest, and BuzzFeed want anything but exclusivity. They want users to share their stories, comment, and make a story "viral," not exclusive. Similarly, prestigious scientific journals like *Nature, Science,* the *New England Journal of Medicine,* or the *Journal of the American Medical Association* want exclusive rights to research publications in order to build their reputation and readership.

---

228    Jeremy Heimans and Henry Timms, *New Power: How Power Works in Our Hyperconnected World—and How to Make It Work for You* (New York: Penguin Random House, 2018), p. 1.

229    Heimans and Timms, *New Power,* 24.

In contrast, open-access scientific journals want scholarly research and literature freely available online to anyone interested in reading it.

Another example of old power versus new power is traditional currency versus cryptocurrency. Old power sees the value of the U.S. dollar as a reflection of the federal government's exclusive ability to print money with the full faith and credit of the government behind it. Cryptocurrencies like Bitcoin are backed by nothing. The value of a Bitcoin is whatever those in the market for Bitcoin say it is. When there is no owner, the crowd must accept whatever the market dictates because the market offers the only legitimate answer as to the value of cryptocurrency.

Old power versus new power confrontations are a source of hate. Not due to a direct confrontation between conservatives and liberals but indirectly in the form of older generations versus younger generations. In a different era, the debate over new power, social media, or cryptocurrency might be just a generational issue like a debate over the Vietnam War, rock 'n roll music, or nuclear arms. In the era of hatred, the debate is impregnated with much more contempt. Contempt has become an easy emotion to express. Mocking others with sarcasm and condescension, hostile humor, name-calling, eye-rolling, and sneering can be done effortlessly online with words and emojis. The net result is that the most fragile are injured by these passive-aggressive acts. Protests can be organized online, but true tyrants with real power don't respond unless they feel consequences in the three-dimensional world.

Even when contempt is unintended, the keyboard is a poor interface for tamping it down. Political opponents are in each other's virtual face constantly. Social media and 24/7 cable news offers space and time to fill with stories about people we want to see in the worst light possible. Our minds are primed to see and hear their hypocrisy. The more we see and hear of them, the more convinced we become of their lunacy.

To paraphrase one of the morals from Aesop's Fables, familiarity and hypocrisy breed contempt.[230]

Liberal hypocrisy is front and center when it comes to tolerance. Tolerance is a word that alienates conservatives. It's a progressive word that is used to describe an ideology that ironically is very intolerant to conservatives, particularly conservatives of faith. Tolerance has become a euphemism for "I like historically marginalized groups." From a conservative point of view, professing tolerance implies being a big enough person to forgive something that is wrong with another person. But if there is nothing wrong with the other person, what exactly is being tolerated? If you don't think it is wrong for someone to change gender based on their feelings, then why would you expect to receive "woke points" for tolerating it? Thus most conservatives see liberals mistaking tolerance for fellowship or tribalism. They believe liberals are standing for something their tribe sees as important, when all they are really doing is affirming feelings they were already supposed to have by virtue of being in the tribe.[231]

Just beneath the argument for tolerance lies the notion that regardless of the grouping, we are all equal. We are not. We are not equally beautiful or strong, gifted or sensible. We are certainly not equally wealthy, and there is no doubt that the child of wealthy parents will have more opportunities than the child of poor parents. Thoughtful conservatives can't just write off all these differences as a matter of social construct—that anyone can be whatever they want to be and that differences are merely the result of environment, opportunity, and privilege. As we work to cleanse our system of real sexism and racism, do we really think all sexual and ethnic

---

230    Aesop, The Fox and the Lion, https://fablesofaesop.com/the-fox-and-the-lion. html

231    French, *Divided We Fall*, 185.

groups are going to choose things in the same proportion? Might there be some differences between the groups that make them more likely to choose a certain profession, prefer competition over cooperation, choose to work with people rather than things, or cope with problems differently?[232]

If the only acceptable end of liberal social policy is equality of outcome, how is such a policy any different in effect than the regimented societies desired by fascist regimes of early twentieth-century Europe? What liberals and progressives see as conventional activism for a righteous cause is perceived as oppression and hatred by conservatives. If the edicts of the woke mob become the only acceptable guides for how society can move forward, conservatives are left with the impression that they are dispensable. When corporations threaten states like Georgia or Indiana for enacting laws against abortion or voter identification but continue to do business with truly oppressive regimes in China and Saudi Arabia, the perception is that they despise their own citizens more than they dislike true tyrants. It's not the sanctions themselves, it's the contempt behind the sanctions.[233] Tolerance is reserved only for those that embrace the liberal agenda.

Those who embrace such an agenda have to be prepared to keep their thinking nimble. The mental calisthenics far-left liberals must go through to stay faithful to their cause can be utterly ridiculous. The first step is to repudiate that which was previously thought to be fixed— like two sexes. Gender is not real but is instead a social construct born from a reiterated social performance. Similarly, race isn't real. It's also a reiterated social performance. The pattern to such mental calisthenics is aided by academia. To deconstruct deeply held beliefs in academia is

---

232 Murray, *The Madness of Crowds*, loc. 3164.

233 French, *Divided We Fall*, 202.

just as important as building something useful in real life. The irony of the deconstruction of thought is that it often leaves a big mess that no one wants to clean up. Gender isn't real until it pits feminists against transgenders. Race isn't real until someone tries to change their race. Sexuality is fluid until it is convenient to argue otherwise. The logic is as convoluted as a Stanley Kubrick film and is the subject of the next chapter.

# CHAPTER 10

★ ★ ★ ★ ★ ★ ★

# SEXUAL IDENTITY, SEXUALITY, INTELLIGENCE, AND RACE

There is a pattern of thought far-left liberals use to protect one group while disparaging another. It begins with a belief that some of the traits and behaviors that comprise human character are genetically hardwired into our DNA and thus are a result of chance, not choice. Other traits and behaviors are the result of some combination of family dynamics, community, and social constructs that are also incidental and beyond an individual's control. One repercussion of believing that these traits and behaviors can not be self-determined is that individuals must be accepted as they are without blame. Provided, of course, that the individual is a member of a protected group.

The liberal pattern of thought continues that there are still other traits and behaviors that are a matter of choice. Irrespective of the consequences, those choices must also be accepted by the rest of us without blame. Provided, of course, that the choice is woke. If the individual is not in a protected group or the choice is not woke, it is open season for the individual to be mocked, ridiculed, or hated. In the fall of 2018, three separate stories made national headlines that, when read together, provide an illustration of this pattern.

After being chastised by conservatives for being overly enthusiastic about her self-proclaimed Native American ancestry, former Democratic presidential candidate and current Massachusetts senator Elizabeth Warren publicly released the results of her genetic ancestry test. To her delight, the test revealed that she indeed had a small amount of Native American ancestry. The two most important words in the previous sentence being "small" and "Native American." Since her DNA sample was compared against test subjects with Mexican, Peruvian, and Colombian ancestry (Native Americans have strong feelings against using their DNA as proof of heritage and thus don't submit their DNA for analysis), many Native Americans denied her assertion that a DNA test was proof that she was part of their community. In addition, the amount of her DNA matching the comparison group was found on only five segments of her genome that may have been inherited 6-10 generations ago."[234] While the amount of Native American DNA senator Warren shares with the comparison group is more than the average European American, many questioned calling out her identification with a culture so far down on her family tree.[235]

---

234    Asma Khalid, "Warren Releases DNA Results, Challenges Trump over Native American Ancestry," NPR.org, October 15, 2018. https://www.npr.org/2018/10/15/657468655/warren-releases-dna-results-challenges-trump-over-native-american-ancestry.

235    Asma Khalid, "Warren Apologizes to Cherokee Nation for DNA Test," NPR.org, February 1, 2019. https://www.npr.org/2019/02/01/690806434/warren-apologizes-to-cherokee-nation-for-dna-test.

The second story came from the world of cycling where a transgender woman, Dr. Rachel McKinnon, won the women's sprint 35–39 age bracket at the Masters Track Cycling World Championships in Los Angeles. Afterward, Dr. McKinnon, who is an assistant professor of philosophy at the College of Charleston, tweeted out her victory, stating she was the "first transgender woman world champion." Third place finisher, Dr. Jennifer Wagner-Assali, an orthopedic surgeon, expressed her displeasure at losing to a biological male by tweeting back "It's definitely NOT fair."[236] Dr. McKinnon was invited to compete in the World Championships thanks to a change in policy regarding testosterone levels in women athletes. In November of 2015, the International Olympic Committee (IOC) changed its policy and allowed transgender women to compete in women's athletic events provided their testosterone level was below 10 nmol/liter for at least twelve months prior to competition (the normal range for women is 0.12 to 1.79 nmol/liter and for men is 7.7 to 29.4 nmol/liter).[237] Thus, in theory and in the spirit of fair competition, any woman, transgender or otherwise, could take testosterone supplements up to the 10 nmol/liter level and still be compliant with IOC rules. Such a possibility must cause Lance Armstrong some pause since he was disgraced and stripped of his Tour de France titles for taking testosterone supplements.[238]

---

236    Alex Ballinger, "Rachel McKinnon becomes first transgender woman to win track world title," October 17, 2018. https://www.cyclingweekly.com/news/latest-news/rachel-mckinnon-becomes-first-transgender-woman-win-track-world-title-397473.

237    Sean Ingle, "IOC delays new transgender guidelines after scientists fail to agree," *The Guardian*, September 24, 2019. https://www.theguardian.com/sport/2019/sep/24/ioc-delays-new-transgender-guidelines-2020-olympics.

238    Owen Gibson, "Lance Armstrong case: The different drugs taken and how they were used," *The Guardian*, October 11, 2012. https://www.theguardian.com/sport/2012/oct/11/lance-armstrong-drugs.

The third story occurred in Federal District Court in Boston where Students for Fair Admission (SFFA), led by a group of Asian Americans who were denied admission to Harvard University, sued the school over its admission policy. The group claimed that Harvard discriminated against them based on their high academic achievement and gave preference to other racial and ethnic minorities (Asian Americans must score around 200 points higher on the Scholastic Aptitude Test (SAT) to be competitive for admission). If the admission policy was based on academic achievement alone, the SFFA showed that the incoming class at Harvard would be 43 percent Asian compared to the 18.66 percent it actually was.[239] The SFFA ultimately lost their case, and the Harvard admission policy continues to include race as one of the factors for evaluating admission candidates. In her ruling on the case, Judge Allison Burroughs wrote, "Race conscious admissions programs that survive strict scrutiny will have an important place in society and help ensure that colleges and universities can offer a diverse atmosphere that fosters learning, improves scholarships, and encourages mutual respect and understanding."[240]

To recap those three stories from the fall of 2018, Native Americans believe genetics *should not* be considered in racial identity; Democratic senator Elizabeth Warren believes it *should*. Cycling champion and transgender woman Dr. Rachel McKinnon believes genetics *should not* be important in determining sex, at least in athletic competitions. Third place finisher Dr. Jennifer Wagner-Assali believes it *should*. Harvard University believes genetics *should be* important in determining

---

239    Scott Jaschik "Judge Upholds Harvard's Admissions Policies," Inside Higher Ed website, October 7, 2019. https://www.insidehighered.com/admissions/article/2019/10/07/federal-judge-finds-harvards-policies-do-not-discriminate-against.

240    Jaschik, "Judge Upholds Harvard's Admissions."

admission to their school, while Asian Americans believe genetics *should not* be considered. Thus we have Native Americans, transgender women cyclists, and Asian Americans on one side *against* the use of genetics to determine an outcome, with Senator Warren, frustrated women cyclists, and Harvard University admissions *for* the use of genetics to determine an outcome. How do we make sense of this?

If we were to be gracious to Senator Warren, perhaps she only wanted to be appreciated for being the authentic version of herself. Maybe she thought genetics made her, ever so slightly, part of the Native American community. Unfortunately for her, she was roundly mocked by the woke virtual mob and had to apologize to Native Americans.[241] Her mistake was in trying to change racial lanes and insert her obvious whiteness into the Native American community. Genetics aside, Senator Warren was not a member of a protected group.

Dr. Wagner-Assali's mistake was going after a transgender female, a member of a highly protected group. Although some transphobic people took the opportunity to make hurtful remarks about Dr. McKinnon,[242] those disgraceful comments distracted from the main issue. Dr. Wagner-Assali was never going to win on her argument that genetics should matter in athletic contests when the virtual mob was there to defend a member of a protected group.

---

241     https://www.nytimes.com/2019/02/01/us/politics/elizabeth-warren-cherokee-dna.html.

242     Meghan DeMaria, "Cycling champion apologizes for transphobic comments after world championship, Yahoo! Life, October 20, 2018. https://www.yahoo.com/lifestyle/cycling-champion-apologizes-transphobic-comments-world-championship-163702548.html.

The SFFA also picked a difficult battle. While Asian Americans are a recognized minority,[243] they suffer from being too good. Their academic prowess, hard work, and resilience makes them a group that is too powerful and not in need of protection by the virtual mob. As Judge Burroughs wrote in her SFFA ruling, race conscious programs are necessary to foster a diverse atmosphere. Apparently, too much of one race, no matter how qualified, throws that atmosphere into chaos. For the young Asian girl who spent her teenage years studying and preparing to go to a great university like Harvard, sorry not sorry.

Of course arguing about whether genetics do or don't matter is silly. Obviously genetics matter. How much they matter depends on the trait being measured. The more complex a human trait, the more genes are involved and the more influential the interaction between genes and environmental conditions involved in developing that trait. This is why geneticists always talk about the contributions of nature *and* nurture when discussing such traits. If we consider a very narrow and well-defined trait like marathon running, genetics matter a lot. The genetically determined long, light frame and deep chest of the East Africans allows them to dominate running marathons. The top ten men's marathon times in history are all East Africans, [244] as well as six of the top ten women's times[245] (three of the top ten non-East African women's times are by the same woman, Paula Radcliffe from Great Britain).

---

243 World Directory of Minorities and Indigenous People, "United States of America Asian Americans," minority rights group international. https://minorityrights.org/minorities/asian-pacific-americans/.

244 "All-time men's best marathon," Track and Field all-time Performances Homepage, October 12, 2021. https://www.alltime-athletics.com/mmaraok.htm.

245 "All-time women's best marathon," Track and Field all-time Performances Homepage, October 12, 2021. http://www.alltime-athletics.com/wmaraok.htm.

On the other hand, wide-ranging behavioral traits like intelligence have some genetic component but are also heavily influenced by social and environmental factors, such as nutrition, surrounding culture, and geography.[246] Intelligence is an ability to adapt to change and accomplish complex goals. There are components of curiosity and persistence wrapped inside of it. It is a combination of verbal, mathematical, musical, athletic, and social aptitude that is malleable with time and experience. Identical twins raised together and identical twins raised apart exhibit a higher correlation between their IQ scores than siblings or fraternal twins raised together, confirming a genetic component to intelligence. At the same time, other psychologists have shown that intelligence is heavily influenced by a child's environment.[247] More accurately, when environmental constraints,—such as an unsupportive family, weak education, or poor nutrition—are removed, the genetics of intelligence gets to play its full hand.

I suspect that even the most liberal crowds care very little about the genetic advantage that East Africans have for marathon running or that tall people have for playing basketball or that short people have for gymnastics. Caucasians, Arabs, and Asians don't get a head start in the marathon ahead of East Africans, short people don't get to dunk on a lower basket, and tall people don't get a handicapped gymnastics score. On the other hand, all of us should care deeply about how people with different levels of intelligence are treated. We would rightly be very upset if those with lower IQ scores weren't given opportunities to have great teachers, adequate resources, and educational opportunities in

---

246 "Is intelligence determined by genetics," Medline plus, https://medlineplus. gov/genetics/understanding/traits/intelligence/.

247 "The Source of Intelligence," lumen website, Introduction to Psychology. https://courses.lumenlearning.com/atd-bhcc-intropsych/chapter/the-source-of-intelligence/.

order to become the best version of themselves. We all have an innate understanding of how complex and important the development of intelligence is for an individual's future.

If we bookend our levels of concern about how genetics should affect athletic performance in specific events on one end and intelligence on the other, it is revealing how we treat issues in between. If an East *Asian* identified themselves as an East *African* and entered a marathon, the claimed change in ethnicity should have no effect on the outcome of the race. If an East Asian claimed to be East African, such a claim wouldn't make them run like an East African. Presumably there would be no consequence because the misidentification would not affect the outcome. Moreover, we instinctively know that no matter how a runner might feel about their ethnicity, it doesn't change anything with regard to their performance. On the other hand, what if a former male runner identified as a female runner and entered the women's marathon race? That would likely affect the outcome. The 4,000th fastest male marathon time is still faster than the world record time for women.[248] There may be requests for a separate race for transgender runners or other races for nonbinary runners. At a minimum, the race officials would have a big public relations issue on their hands as the virtual mob would presumably weigh in, just as they did with Dr. McKinnon in the 2018 Cycling World Championships.

Before going further, I want to acknowledge that sex determination is not as straightforward or binary as what most of us learned in high school biology. Briefly, that lesson was that when egg meets sperm, each parent contributes twenty-two non-sex chromosomes and one sex chromosome—an X from the mother and either an X or Y from the father. The presence of a gene called SRY (sex-determining region Y

---

248    "All-time men's best marathon," Track and Field.

chromosome) on the Y chromosome initiates the release of testosterone and the formation of male sex organs while the baby is growing inside the mother's uterus. Absent an SRY gene, the baby will develop female sex organs. That is if everything goes according to plan.

There are a number of disorders of sexual development (DSD) that affect around 1 in 4,500 to 5,500 births when things don't go according to plan.[249] Due to small changes in the genetic code in those disorders, testosterone is either synthesized incorrectly or does not have the intended action on other cells. Thus, babies with the XY sex chromosomes of a male can have female genitalia. In other cases, babies with the XX sex chromosomes of a female can have small genetic errors that cause over secretion of adrenal hormones that result in a masculine body type and ambiguous genitalia. There are other syndromes and genetic variations that can also make sexual identity less than straightforward. Thus, making sweeping statements about there only being two sexes is not accurate. Exceptions exist and sex determination is sometimes complex. Most importantly, individuals with these genetic variations deserve just as much dignity as those who don't, and reasonable accommodations should be made for their unique circumstances. At the same time, it is also important to keep in mind that those cases are rare and unusual.

There is an adage in the legal field that extreme cases make for bad law. It is meant as a caution to lawmakers and judges that rare and unusual cases are a poor basis for a general law that should cover a wide range of similar but less extreme cases. For example, it would be senseless for a city to change its building code to require all doorways to be at least eight feet high because 0.000038 percent of the population is over seven

---

249    A. Bashamboo and K. McElreavey, "Mechanism of Sex Determination in Humans: Insights from Disorders of Sex Development," Karger, 2016. https://www.karger.com/Article/Fulltext/452637.

feet tall and needs the extra door height.[250] Liberal thinking often sets that adage aside. In a much criticized article on banning transgender athletes from competing in women's sports, *CNN* reporter Devan Cole claimed, "It's not possible to know a person's gender identity at birth, and for some people, the sex listed on their original birth certificate is a misleading way of describing the body they have."[251] Cole goes on in the article to write "while sex is a category that refers broadly to physiology, a person's gender is an innate sense of identity."

His comments reflect a liberal ideology that feelings are facts, not opinions offered up for interpretation. That ideology is reflected in population studies. Despite DSDs occurring in roughly 1 in 5,000 births (less often than the lifetime likelihood of being struck by lightning) in population studies,[252] more than four times that number identify as being nonbinary,[253] leading to the conclusion that many people simply identify as nonbinary not because of their genetics but because of how they feel. On an individual basis, the notion that gender is not just biological but rather a complex interaction between genetics and environment is not disruptive. Gender is a very personal and private matter. But when an individual is free to change their gender because of how they feel, a protected group is given special privileges that the rest of

---

250    "How Many 7 Footers Are in the World?" Percentage Calculator. https://percentagecalculator.mes.fm/interesting-facts/how-many-7-footers-are-in-the-world#.

251    Devon Cole, "South Dakota's governor issues executive orders banning transgender athletes from women's sports," *CNN*, March 31, 2021. https://www.*CNN*.com/2021/03/30/politics/south-dakota-transgender-sports-kristi-noem/index.html.

252    Desirée O, 50 "Rare" Events That Happen All the Time," Bestlife, July 15, 2020. https://bestlifeonline.com/rare-events/.

253    Fiona Glen and Karen Hurrell, *Technical note: Measuring Gender Identity* (Manchester, UK: Equality and Human Rights Commission, 2012).

us are expected to honor. Each individual has the liberty to ignore their biological reality, but what is the compelling reason that the rest of us must also ignore the same reality? Should a gynecologist be compelled to see a genetic male who insists on being treated like a female? How is recognizing the biological reality of sex different than recognizing the reality of age, height, or weight? If a 5 ft., 3 in., 250 pound man joins a pickup basketball game and claims to be 6 ft., 8 in., and 200 pounds, should the team be compelled to play him at center because that's where the man says he feels most comfortable?

The suggestion that gender is a pattern of reiterated social performance and not biologically fixed is also disruptive to feminism. When anyone who feels female can be a female, genetics aside, who is Title IX,[254] a federal program to equalize the money colleges and universities have for men's and women's activities, supposed to help? A gender fluid environment creates an expectation to disregard the conventional golden rule of "do unto others as you would have them do unto you"[255] and invoke the platinum rule of "do unto others as they want done to them."[256] Why? Because they feel special and deserve more privilege than those who are not gender fluid? Never mind that members of a non-protected group can experience disrespect but are expected to accept that treatment as a consequence of their powerful, oppressive nature, sex, or race.

---

254 Title IX is part of the Education Amendments Act of 1972 that precludes colleges and universities from discriminating against women.

255 Brannon Deibert, "What is the Golden Rule?—Biblical Meaning, Importance and Examples, Christianity.com, February 12, 2019. https://www.christianity.com/christian-life/what-is-the-golden-rule.html.

256 Gordon C. Nagayama Hal, "The Platinum Rule," *Psychology Today*, February 7, 2017. https://www.psychologytoday.com/us/blog/life-in-the-intersection/201702/the-platinum-rule.

In a similar manner, liberals submit that sexual orientation is *not* fixed but also "fluid," albeit with more objective data to explain what that means. Studies on homosexual identical and fraternal twins show that identical twins are more likely to both be gay than fraternal twins. But when an older brother is gay, it is more likely that a younger brother will also be gay. Thus, there is very likely a genetic component to homosexuality, but because sexuality is a spectrum of preferences and behaviors, the interaction between genetics and environment is complex and not completely understood.[257] Sexually fluid people tend to experience attractions at different points along the spectrum as they go through life. "Fluidity is an absolutely normal aspect of sexual orientation," explains Will Zogg, a Washington therapist who specializes in gender affirming counseling. "Attraction is far more complex than many people can communicate."[258]

But if gender is an "innate sense of identity" and sexual attraction is "far more complex than many people can communicate," why doesn't the same flexibility apply to race? Rather than submitting genetics as evidence of race like Senator Warren, could one define their own race based on that same "innate sense of identity"? Rachel Dolezal tried. Ms. Dolezal was a white woman born to white parents in Montana in 1977. By her own account, she never felt white. She felt Black. She imagined that she was an Egyptian princess separated from her true family at birth. After graduating from high school, she moved to Jackson, Mississippi, became close with Black religious leaders there, applied bronzer to her face, braided her hair in a traditional Afro

---

257     Adam Rutherford, *Humanimal: How Homo sapiens Became Nature's Most Paradoxical Creature—A New Evolutionary History* (New York: The Experiment, 2019), p. 130.

258     Crystal Raypole, "What Does It Mean to Be Sexually Fluid," Healthline, December 22, 2020. https://www.healthline.com/health/sexually-fluid#definition.

look, and created a new life. She went on to become a professor of Black studies at Eastern Washington University, was the president of the Spokane, Washington, chapter of the National Association for the Advancement of Colored People (NAACP), and sat on Spokane's police accountability commission. Then on June 11, 2015, while doing a television interview, she was asked by the interviewer if she was African American. She responded by saying she didn't understand the question. Shortly thereafter, Ms. Dolezal's parents came forward and exposed her actual race. Within the day, she was labeled as a "race faker," derided for dressing in "blackface," fired from her jobs, kicked off the police accountability commission, and lost nearly all her friends and colleagues while her son received text messages stating, "Tell your mom to kill herself and do the world a favor."[259]

Thus in the liberal mind, gender fluid men and women should be regarded as whatever sex their "innate sense of identity" tells them. On the other hand, people trying to cross racial lines do not receive the same warm welcome. The tortured logic being that if you didn't grow up Black, you cannot understand what being Black means, which is apparently very different from understanding what it is like to be a woman if you have previously been a man. How do we make sense of this?

The answer is not complicated. Human beings decide emotionally and justify logically. Our primal, impassioned temporal lobes of the brain and deep-seated portions of the brainstem come up with answers and ask our more sophisticated frontal and parietal lobes to come up with a reason. Julius Caesar said it more vividly, "What we wish, we readily

259    Chris McGreal, "Rachel Dolezal: I wasn't identifying as black to upset people. I was being me," *The Guardian*, December 13, 2015. https://www.theguardian.com/us-news/2015/dec/13/rachel-dolezal-i-wasnt-identifying-as-black-to-upset-people-i-was-being-me.

believe, and what we ourselves think, we imagine others think also."[260] Logic is merely a sidecar to the engine of emotion. It is the same tactic used by liberals to create the change they seek in the world around them. If you cannot rule a society or pretend to rule it, then the next best thing is to play on the emotions of the masses and spread doubt about everything. Make people doubt that the society they live in is good. Make them doubt they are treated fairly. Make them doubt that there is a physical difference between women and men. Make them doubt that gender and sexuality are not fixed but fluid. Make them doubt everything, and then assert that you have the answers.[261]

When the same tactic of spreading doubt is applied retrospectively, history gets rewritten. The fallacy in rewriting history from the present is that whoever is doing the rewriting thinks they would have behaved better than the historical figures involved. They would have ended slavery sooner, passed women's suffrage earlier, prevented Japanese internment during World War II, and acted against Jim Crow laws. Of course, they only think they would have acted better because we already know how the history turned out. The characters of history did not have that luxury.

To view the past with some degree of forgiveness is an early request to be forgiven in turn.[262] The behaviors we exhibit today will not survive the future whirlwind of retribution and judgment. For example, given the growing backlash against humans eating meat, it is possible that future generations will look back at our own generation with disgust knowing that we raised, butchered, and ate animals. As we anthropomorphize

---

260    Julius Caesar quote. Reddit. https://www.reddit.com/r/quotes/comments/8k6a4w/what_we_wish_we_readily_believe_and_what_we/.

261    Murray, *The Madness of Crowds*, loc. 4679.

262    Murray, *The Madness of Crowds*, loc. 3369.

dogs, cows, tigers, lions, pumas, elephants, and dozens of other animals, it is possible that future generations will look back with revulsion that we "owned" animals and kept them in our homes, farms, or zoos under anything less than human conditions.

For a present day example, we don't need to look any further than gay rights over the last few generations. Nineteenth-century laws banned homosexual conduct as a "crime against nature."[263] The criminalization of homosexual acts continued through the latter half of the twentieth century as the U.S. Supreme Court upheld the constitutionality of laws banning homosexual acts in 1986 in *Bowers v. Hardwick*.[264] Finally, in the 2003 case of *Lawrence v. Texas*, the Bowers decision was reversed, and laws banning homosexual conduct were deemed unconstitutional.

Looking back from the perspective of today, such laws make it seem like nineteenth- and twentieth-century America was a foreign country. But it would be extremely unforgiving to judge every adult living prior to 2003 who didn't stand up against anti-homosexual laws as evil. The prevailing view on homosexuality was based on hundreds of years of habit and custom. The U.S. Supreme Court reflected that view in its reasoning of *Bowers v. Hardwick*, noting that states had laws banning homosexual conduct since the nation's founding, and thus, there could be no protected fundamental right to engage in such acts. But the culture changed. Homosexuality is not seen in the same historical light, and while the road to creating change was difficult and violent at times, is it necessary to hate the people who didn't advocate for change?

---

263    Richard Weinmeyer, "The Decriminalization of Sodomy in the United States, *AMA Journal of Ethics,* November 2014. https://journalofethics.ama-assn.org/article/decriminalization-sodomy-united-states/2014-11.

264    Weinmeyer, "The Decriminalization of Sodomy."

Eighteenth-century philosopher Cesare Beccaria once wrote, "Happy is the nation without a history."[265] He described how forgetfulness and historical error are necessary in building a nation. A nation that feels guilty for every evil it has committed will lack the energy and conviction to defend itself. A thorough retelling of a nation's history undermines the bonds produced by a proud collective memory. For example, Americans have a romantic account of the American Revolution, while the British see it as a rebel uprising made possible by the French. "History is mostly guesswork, the rest is just prejudice,"[266] said the great historian Will Durant. Much like we use logic to justify our emotions, we use our prejudice to rewrite the history we prefer to believe. If you choose to look at the past through the lens of race, every powerful person was racist and every decision that hurt Black people was racially motivated. If you are an economist, you look back at those same people and decisions and see the result of incentives and penalties. If you are a psychologist, you see the consequences of bias and prejudice. The past gains significance only once a culture's habits and customs are formed and have to be justified.

History is more complex and opaque than we are willing to acknowledge. We know the outcome but not the script that produces the outcome. In retrospect, the outcome seems like a foregone conclusion because we can see the historical pattern. Today, laws like ones that criminalized homosexual conduct seem archaic and completely out of touch with our reality. But thirty-five years ago, reality was very different. From the perspective of someone living in 1986 with hundreds of years of history filled with laws preventing homosexual conduct, foreseeing those laws would be struck down and American culture would become accepting of homosexual conduct and gay marriage within a generation was

---

265    Moffett, *The Human Swarm*, 198.

266    Durant, *The Lessons of History*, loc. 30.

impossible. No one could have known how activists for gay rights, the AIDS epidemic, art, music, theater, and literature would successfully communicate the need for cultural change. The reality we have now was one of many possible futures thirty-five years ago. Destiny only becomes destiny after it arrives.

But the story of gay rights in this country is not unique in regards to the timing of how it happened. History does not crawl; it makes jumps. Progress comes in small spurts intermixed with setbacks and failures until one day there is a marked change. Today, as far-left liberals rewrite the history of slavery, women's rights, Jim Crow, and oppression of homosexuals, the corollary has become that white people must be much worse than previously thought. It was white people who were the majority and used their power to target minorities, women, homosexuals, and anyone else that didn't bend to the will of the white majority. As an illustration, it has been illegal to pay women less for the same job in the U.S. since 1963. Despite that, seven out of ten people think women are not paid the same amount for doing the same job as men.[267] While acknowledging that payroll sexism still offensively occurs in some organizations, it has been illegal to do so for nearly sixty years. Similarly, it has been illegal to discriminate based on race, color, religion, sex, or national origin for purposes of hiring, firing, or promoting since 1964, yet one in four Americans believe discrimination is based in government laws and policies.[268]

Revising history changes the perspective of generations who didn't live through that period of history. Firsthand accounts get drowned out

---

267   Murray, *The Madness of Crowds*, loc. 4579.

268   Joel Neel, "Poll: Most Americans Think Their Own Group Faces Discrimination," NPR.org, October 24, 2017. https://www.npr.org/sections/health-shots/2017/10/24/559116373/poll-most-americans-think-their-own-group-faces-discrimination.

by the narrative that fits how revisionists want the particular historical period to be remembered. The consequence of drowning out those accounts and rewriting history to arrive at a particular conclusion is another source of hate. It disregards the experiences and perspectives of those with different beliefs. That is the topic of our next chapter.

# CHAPTER 11

★ ★ ★ ★ ★ ★ ★

# THIS IS NOT NEW

The American Midwest and its coasts are geographically a half continent apart, but culturally, they can feel halfway around the world. The pace of life for those of us in the Midwest is a bit slower. Less urgency means friendships have time to form, even with total strangers, leaving visitors with the feeling of "Midwest nice." There is a sense of humility that comes from knowing the world's epicenter lies elsewhere. Trends and fads are less impactful with more value placed on what has worked in the past. Greater physical distance between people means ethnic groups mix less. Families of Swedish Minnesotans and Czech Nebraskans who have lived in the same areas for generations have little cause to mingle. Midwesterners tend to pay less attention to people that try hard to have attention paid to them. It is a place where heart-warming tales about average Americans, folksy observations, and old-fashioned plain talk are valued. I suspect that if most Hollywood celebrities were to make an appearance in the small and medium-sized towns of the Midwest, few would show up to meet them. There would be exceptions. Springfield,

Missouri, is exceptionally proud of its most popular son, Brad Pitt. In his prime, Johnny Carson, a proud Nebraska native, would have drawn a huge crowd, as would radio broadcaster and Presidential Medal of Freedom recipient Paul Harvey. From 1951 to 2008, Paul Harvey programs reached as many as twenty-four million people per week. Paul Harvey News was carried on 1,200 radio stations, 400 American Forces Network stations, and in 300 newspapers.[269] His folksy, seesaw baritone voice was punctuated by long pauses that kept generations of Midwesterners entertained twice a day, once over lunch and again in the afternoon on the way home from work or the fields. Mr. Harvey worried about the national debt, big government, bureaucrats who lacked common sense, permissive parents, leftist radicals, and America succumbing to moral decay. He championed rugged individualism, love of God and country, and the fundamental decency of ordinary people. He saw Americans through the Korean and Vietnam Wars, the Cuban missile crisis, a presidential assassination and another attempt, trips to the moon, and exploding space shuttles. His daily presence made people feel normal in times that felt very abnormal. When anxiety peaked, he was calm. "In times like these it helps to recall that there have always been times like these,"[270] he once told his concerned audience. Mr. Harvey passed away in 2009, but if he were alive today, he would remind us that extremism, racism, nativism, and isolation, driven by fear of the unknown, tends to spike in periods of economic and social stress—much like the one we are in now.

---

269  Wikipedia, "Paul Harvey." https://en.wikipedia.org/wiki/Paul_Harvey.

270  Paul Harvey, quote, Goodreads. https://www.goodreads.com/quotes/51252-in-times-like-these-it-is-helpful-to-remember-that.

To deal with anxiety, we try to understand what is going on around us and anticipate what might happen next. The best insights do not come from observing current events or even reflecting on our most recent history. The best insights come from the distant past. As the great Midwest Missourian Mark Twain allegedly said, "History doesn't repeat itself, but it often rhymes."

Looking to the distant past for possible insights into our future is not natural. Our brains suffer from recency bias. We favor the lessons of recent events over historic ones. We consider everything around when we were born as normal and ordinary, everything invented between the ages of fifteen and thirty-five as new and exciting, and everything invented after the age of thirty-five as against the natural order of things.[271] The technology, ideas, and events that predate our lives are part of a different world. What happened to other people in the distant past and the lessons learned from those experiences feels less relevant than what we have experienced and learned during our own lifetime. Unfortunately, that bias leaves big gaps in our anticipation for the future. The big events of history that hold the most valuable insights, plagues and pandemics come to mind, occur only once every few generations. For example, the skepticism and fear of COVID-19 vaccines had its beginnings with the invention of vaccines. The first inoculation against smallpox in the 1720s was decried as antithetical to God's will and raised the issue of balancing individual liberty with caring for the public's health.[272] As the memories of those events fade, our brains find reasons why the lessons learned don't apply. "While the lessons and warnings of history are clear

---

271    Rutherford, *Humanimal,* 21.

272    Alicia Ault, "History Shows Americans Have Always Been Wary of Vaccines," Simthsonianmag.com, January 26, 2012.  https://www.smithsonianmag.com/smithsonian-institution/history-shows-americans-have-always-been-wary-vaccines-180976828/

if one looks for them, most people don't look for them because most people learn from their experiences, and a single lifetime is too short to give them those lessons and warnings that they need,"[273] observed investor Ray Dalio.

If we can suspend our recency bias and look back over several thousand years of time, our current economic and social stressors are less novel. We are living in the beginning of a third economic revolution—the Digital Revolution. The two prior revolutions, agricultural and industrial, were equally tumultuous. The Agricultural Revolution began around 10,000 BC when humans transitioned from hunting and gathering to the domestication of crops and livestock. Ninety percent of the foodstuffs that feed us today, including cattle, sheep, goats, wheat, rice, corn, potatoes, millet, and barley, were domesticated around that time.[274] The transition was not smooth. Being able to produce more food and energy allowed for larger groups of people to live together in towns and cities. But there was a price to pay for the added productivity. Initially, people became smaller, weaker, and more sickly, as crops sometimes failed due to drought or pestilence and livestock succumbed to disease or nature's will. The trend of smaller, more sickly people continued until the invention of the plow and harnessed oxen of the Roman era.[275] Thus, for the first 10,000 years of agriculture, its essence was to keep more people alive under worse conditions. During the Agricultural Revolution, power was determined by the amount of land one controlled. More land meant more production and wealth, resulting in conflicts large and small waged over the control of the best lands.

---

273    Ray Dalio, "Study History," Investment Master Class website. http://mastersinvest.com/historyquotes.

274    Yuval Noah Harari, *Sapiens: A Brief History of Humankind* (New York: Harper Collins, 2015), p. 77.

275    Moffett, *The Human Swarm*, 153.

The mid-eighteenth century saw the beginning of the Industrial Revolution with the invention of mechanized spinning and weaving. Mechanization increased the annual economic growth rate in European countries by a factor of ten and increased annual income as well, but it also caused considerable anxiety amongst workers.[276] Mechanized spinning and weaving displaced human workers, including a group named after a young apprentice weaver named Ned Ludd.[277] Feeling their jobs were being forever threatened, the Luddites went around destroying mechanical looms in England. While today their name is associated with those who fear new technology, the Luddites weren't against technology; they just wanted to save their jobs.[278]

The Industrial Revolution progressed through the nineteenth century with the spread of steam engines and railroads followed by the discovery of oil and the use of mass production. Unemployment during the Industrial Revolution did not change, but the transition from an agricultural to a manufacturing economy was not smooth. During the years of 1760 to 1820, diets were poorer, infant mortality increased, and life expectancy fell.[279] Trains and steam engines knit new markets together as the biggest threat to humanity became pneumonia due to the packed urban areas described in Charles Dickens's novels.[280] By the arrival of the mid-twentieth century, manufacturing productivity

---

276    Klaus Schwab and Nicholas David, *Shaping the Fourth Industrial Revolution* (Cologny/Geneva, Switzerland: World Economic Forum, 2018), p. 8.

277    Evan Andrews, "Who Were the Luddites," History.com, June 26, 2019. https://www.history.com/news/who-were-the-luddites.

278    Kevin Ashton, *How to Fly a Horse: The Secret History of Creation, Invention, and Discovery* (New York: Random House, 2015), loc. 1418, Kindle.

279    Susskind, *World Without Work*, 18.

280    Joshua Cooper Ramo, *The Seventh Sense*: Power, Fortune, and Survival in the Age of Networks (New York: Hachette, 2016), p. 19.

had increased to the point that per capita incomes were thirty to one hundred times what they were in 1800.[281] But the added productivity in factories and on farms also made the world's two deadliest wars possible, caused overspeculation in the stock market, and depleted the world's most fertile soils. As French poet Paul Virilio once wrote, "When you invent the ship, you also invent the shipwreck."[282] Power during the Industrial Revolution was defined by the productivity that could be coaxed from factories and workers. Larger factories and more workers resulted in more wealth, resulting in conflicts waged over control of the people and resources that could lead to greater industrial output.

The Industrial Revolution also brought about the first globalization period from 1870 to 1913. During those years, roads were being paved, and the Suez Canal was built, bringing Asia 4,000 miles closer to Europe. Price differentials between cities around the world for commodities from bacon to rice and cotton shrunk from 90 percent to 20 percent.[283] It was also a time of stock markets rising on rapidly expanding technologies like railroads, radio, and telephones. Railway stocks comprised 60 percent of the U.S. stock market value. Much like the period of globalism we experienced in the early twenty-first century, tariffs, economic decline, nationalism, and war also brought down the first era of globalism.[284] Yet another example of history's rhythmic pattern.

The third economic revolution, the Digital Revolution, began in the 1980s following the creation of the internet. Initially, the disruption and unrest created by digital transformation accelerated the loss of manufacturing jobs as automation and robots replaced blue-collar

---

281    Schwab and David, *Shaping the Fourth*, 18.

282    Ramo, *The Seventh Sense*, 36.

283    O'Sullivan, *The Levelling*, 62.

284    O'Sullivan, *The Levelling*, 64.

jobs. Meanwhile, white-collar jobs boomed in service areas, such as healthcare, IT, entertainment, and consulting. Later, social media and the "internet of things" began to connect people and devices, creating a constant stream of data capable of replacing the mental labor of some white-collar workers. With that progression, college graduates and decision makers began displaying more public anxiety about the Digital Revolution. Books, articles, and op-eds began to be written about the ills of big data, automation, and artificial intelligence. Digital innovations have disrupted traditional notions of power and stability in the same way domesticated crops and livestock, oil, engines, and mass production did in the two prior revolutions.

In the Digital Revolution, knowledge and connection elevates power. The knowledge and information we hold projects expertise in a way that only digital connection can leverage. Markets for digital solutions are not just local or regional but, with the ease of virtual connection, can quickly become global, with distribution costs approaching zero. Conflicts that once raged over control of land, resources, and labor are now over who possesses the knowledge and connection. If a terrorist wanted to control Silicon Valley, the way to do so is not to hijack all the silicon—it is the knowledge and connection centered there that is valuable. The implications of a Digital Revolution that favors connection and mental capacity over physical labor are no more or less disruptive than those caused by the Agricultural and Industrial Revolutions.

Connection and the power it represents creates new rules for who benefits from technology and how those benefits are distributed. Unlike physical connection, virtual connection is not bound by traditional borders. This means that those who can harness technology and create powerful connections do not have to be in the same geographic area. Thus, while wealth differences between countries are falling, inequalities within countries are rising.[285] Wealth is being concentrated by economic class but, at the same time, is dispersed over a greater geographical area.

That may seem to be cause for concern, but inequality has always been the handmaiden of progress. Only when a few people become better off does a higher standard of living for the many become imaginable. History offers us examples. Early in the Industrial Revolution, income inequality began to increase as Western Europe and North America industrialized quickly. But in the 1980s, that inequality began to reverse as non-Western countries industrialized and caught up, raising their standard of living and putting many American manufacturers out of business.[286] Likewise, as the Digital Revolution has progressed, countries such as Korea, Singapore, and Finland have strategically invested in infrastructure that has surpassed early digital adopters, like the United States and Western Europe.[287]

The Digital Revolution has also coincided with Americans, as well as the rest of the world, living closer together. Between 1950 and 2018, the percentage of people worldwide living in urban areas went from 29 percent to 55 percent.[288] Over that same period of time, urban dwellers

---

285    Schwab and David, *Shaping the Fourth*, 13.

286    Bailey and Tupy, *Ten Global Trends*, 33.

287    Oliver Reynolds, "Which countries are the most prepared for the upcoming Digital Revolution?" FOCUSECONOMICS, June 7, 2018. https://www.focus-economics.com/blog/what-countries-most-prepared-for-upcoming-digital-revolution.

288    Bailey and Tupy, *Ten Global Trends*, 18.

in the United States went from 64 percent[289] to 82.3 percent.[290] As we have just experienced during the COVID-19 pandemic, physical proximity to one another can be as much of a risk in the twenty-first century as it was during the Dickensian nineteenth century and the era of bacterial pneumonia—not only because of the petri dish created by packing people closely together but because of the cultural mash-up that ensues. The incorporation of massive numbers of different peoples has been the most radical innovation in the history of human societies. Countries as small as Lichtenstein and as large as China are all admixtures of different types of people. The admixture of different races, religions, beliefs, sexualities, and standards naturally creates friction. It is not a coincidence that the most ethnically diverse countries in the world—such as the African countries of Uganda, Liberia, and Rwanda; many Central American countries; Middle Eastern countries including Syria, Jordan, and Iran; and the United States—are areas with the greatest racial and ethnic conflict.[291] In contrast, more ethnically homogenous countries like Japan, Korea, Chile, Argentina, and much of western Europe have less racial conflict.

History offers examples of great world powers that struggled with similar friction. For 2,500 years, every global power has faced the same paradox: to be tolerant enough to attract the brightest minds regardless of race,

---

289    "Urban and rural populations in the United States," Our World in Data website. https://ourworldindata.org/grapher/urban-and-rural-populations-in-the-united-states?time=1950..latest&country=~USA.

290    Aaron A. O'Neill, Urbanization in the United States 1970–1920, statista, July 21, 2021. https://www.statista.com/statistics/269967/urbanization-in-the-united-states/.

291    Max Fisher, "A Revealing Map of the World's Most and Least Ethnically Diverse Countries", *The Washington Post*, May 16, 2013. https://www.washingtonpost.com/news/worldviews/wp/2013/05/16/a-revealing-map-of-the-worlds-most-and-least-ethnically-diverse-countries/.

religion, creed, or color in order to work toward the best interests of society while at the same time forging strong bonds within the group to secure their loyalty.[292] This paradox was the struggle for the Romans, the Mongol Empire of Genghis Khan, and the Dutch and British empires as they tried to incorporate diverse cultures from across Europe, Asia, and Africa. Some were more successful than others. The Romans got people to coexist by exporting technology like plumbing to conquered lands. The Chinese did it by forcing conquered lands to adopt their culture through violence. But to attain and maintain dominance on a global scale, coercion was simply too inefficient, persecution too costly, and ethnic or religious homogeneity, like inbreeding, too unproductive.[293] Mixing people of various races, religions, and ethnicities takes patience, some degree of tolerance, and a deft political hand.

As the number of democracies increase around the world, there is a growing realization that the freedoms democracy offers produces many desirable consequences but that it is also steeped in inequality of outcome. Aristotle warned that inequality brought instability,[294] and that is exactly what is happening. It is more common for democracies to wither away from instability on the inside than from external forces tearing it down from outside. Since the end of the Cold War, most democracies have not died at the hands of soldiers but by the government itself. Venezuela, Georgia, Hungary, Nicaragua, Peru, Philippines, Poland, Russia, Sri Lanka, Turkey, and the Ukraine have all become autocracies in this way.[295]

---

292    Amy Chua, *Day of Empire: How Hyperpowers Rise to Global Dominance—and Why They Fall* (New York: Random House, 2007), loc. 178, Kindle.

293    Chua, *Day of Empire*, loc. 224.

294    Timothy Snyder, *On Tyranny: Twenty Lessons from the Twentieth Century* (New York: Crown, 2017), p. 9.

295    Levitsky and Ziblatt, *How Democracies Die*, 4.

The unwritten rules of a democracy are crucial to its survival. There must be degrees of mutual tolerance and institutional forbearance. Mutual tolerance means that as long as rivals play by the rules, they can exist and compete with one another—to agree to disagree. Forbearance means that those in power will not utilize all of their political power to crush their opponents,[296] but rather will allow them to live to fight another day. Polarization can destroy those democratic norms. When societies sort themselves into political camps that are mutually exclusive, tolerance is hard to sustain. Some polarization is healthy in a democracy, but when societies become so deeply divided that they do not share a common worldview and rarely interact, they begin to see each other as mutual threats. Politicians begin to try to win at all costs and reject democratic norms. When this happens, democracy is in trouble.[297]

Apart from some historical guilt, there is no evidence that any other democratic society in any epoch of history has had some social grace that twenty-first century Americans lack. There is no evidence that primitive societies lived without sexism or homophobia. There is no time in history in any place that was free of racism, transphobia, and full of peace. If you claim that racism, sexism, or homophobia is worse now than it has ever been, then you have a lot of proving to do.[298]

The same historical comparison holds up if we confine our retrospective view to the brief history of the United States. We have always had conflict in this country. Like every culture, the United States struggles with its own fundamental contradiction. Americans value liberty, the freedom to do as one pleases, while at the same time, we desire equality. More freedom means that by talent, effort, or luck, resources become

---

296    Levitsky and Ziblatt, *How Democracies Die,* 100.

297    Levitsky and Ziblatt, *How Democracies Die,* 114.

298    Murray, *The Madness of Crowds,* loc. 4703.

concentrated in the hands of a few. The rate of the concentration of wealth among a few accelerates with the economic freedom that is in inherent tension with the desire for equality.

This inherent tension is present in the two founding documents of American government. The Declaration of Independence displays a clear conviction that the yoke of oppression would be cast aside, and the only source of power would come from the people. On the other hand, the Constitution was a protection against the American people turning into a mob and exerting their will on one another. Thus, nearly a decade after the Declaration of Independence, the Constitution was written as a control on the passions of the public to regulate itself.[299] The Declaration of Independence was about freedom, while the Constitution was about preserving equality.

Ever since the Constitution was written, Americans have been at odds over what "equal" should mean. Racism, sexism, and homophobia have always been part of that debate and likely will be for the duration of our republic. Those who find perpetual arguing stressful or otherwise unsettling should consider finding another country. The government of Madison's architecture was designed to elevate and refine public opinion so that future generations would stay engaged in the debate.

At times, just like today, that debate turned violent. From 1830 to 1860, there were 125 violent acts against members of Congress by members of Congress, including stabbing, caning, and pulling pistols.[300] From 1861 to 1865, the Civil War claimed the lives of 750,000 Americans

---

299   Chua and Rubenfeld, *The Triple Package*, 206.

300   Levitsky and Ziblatt, *How Democracies Die,* 122.

fighting over whether equality included ethnic Africans.[301] Violence continued throughout the Great Depression, the era of Jim Crow, and the civil rights movement as dozens of protestors died over the fight for equality.[302]

The Prussian military genius Carl von Clausewitz called war the "continuation of policy by other means."[303] Once talking and listening becomes futile, the only option left is violence. Violence is a result, not a reason. With time and experience, Americans—as well as most of the rest of the world—are less prone to settling our differences with violence. Historically, wars claimed 10 percent to 60 percent of all men. In the twentieth and twenty-first centuries, it has become a single digit blip.[304] We have become smarter, more understanding, better able to adapt.

What makes us so adaptable is our culture—our ability to copy, imitate, modify, share, and improve. Ideas can move quickly from person to person. Human beings are the only animals that use accumulated knowledge from their ancestors rather than just their DNA. Nurture is

---

301    Daniel Nasaw, "Who, What, Why: How many soldiers died in the U.S. Civil War?" BBC News, April 4, 2012. https://www.bbc.com/news/magazine-17604991#:~:text=For%20more%20than%20a%20century,number%20underrepresented%20the%20death%20toll.

302    Southern Poverty Law Center, "Civil Rights Martyrs," SPLC website. https://www.splcenter.org/what-we-do/civil-rights-memorial/civil-rights-martyrs.

303    Robert Callum, "War as a Continuation of Policy by Other Means: Clausewitzian Theory in the Middle East, *Defense Analysis* 17 no. 1 (2010), 59–72. https://www.tandfonline.com/doi/abs/10.1080/07430170120041802?journalCode=cdan19#:~:text=In%20Clausewitz's%20most%20famous%20words,carried%20on%20with%20other%20means.

304    Murray, *The Madness of Crowds*, loc. 4728.

our nature.[305] Our adaptability means the world has less permanence. In just our lifetime, consider the former truths that simply haven't continued to be true. In the 1980s, Japan was going to dominate the world's economy due to their manufacturing prowess and management practices. In the 1970s, the encyclopedia was the most important and reliable source of knowledge. For most of the nineteenth and twentieth centuries, every major city had one morning and one afternoon newspaper in addition to a few radio and television stations that most thought would last in perpetuity. Even the labels we place on each other change. In the early twentieth century, Italians, Poles, and Jews were not considered white, while the British considered Africans, Indians, and Pakistanis Black.[306]

Change is the one historical constant. In the prior millennium, China was conquered by the Mongols, but one hundred years later during the Ming Dynasty, the Chinese recaptured their country and made it the center of innovation and technology.[307] By 1800, China produced 40 percent of the world economy, but by 1950, it was down to 10 percent.[308] Between 1750 and 1950, Western Europe ascended through the economic boom brought about by imperialism, but it was an imperialism unlike any other in history. Previous empires assumed they understood the world and needed to spread their view to foreign lands and people. Europeans were also driven by the desire to gain new knowledge, as opposed to just

---

305    Ian Leslie, *Curious: The De*sire to Know and Why Your Future Depends on It (New York, Basic Books, 2014) p. 16.

306    Moffett, *The Human Swarm*, 185.

307    Chua and Rubenfeld, *The Triple Package*, 21.

308    O'Sullivan, *The Levelling*, 288.

gaining power and wealth. They not only wanted new territories but new knowledge.[309] They were prepared to adapt.

Today, cycles of business, technology, and politics are short, typically about five years. Any forecasts that look beyond five or ten years are likely to be upended. With such impermanence, talk of an Asian or African century is nonsense. The longer a streak lasts, the less likely it is to continue, and it becomes time to start looking for reasons for the cycle to end. In 2006, 52 percent of Americans thought it was important for a male and female couple to be legally married. By 2013, that had fallen to 40 percent. In 2004, 30 percent of Americans favored allowing same-sex marriage, and 60 percent opposed, but by 2016, 55 percent favored and 35 percent opposed.[310] Nothing is permanent. We have always and will always be in a state of change.

It is disheartening to look around today and see racism, sexism, transphobia, violence, and hatred for one another. Video of liberals using violence against conservatives to suppress their views is just as demoralizing as conservatives scaling the walls of the U.S. Capitol to wrest power from liberals. But to paraphrase Paul Harvey, in times like these, it is important to remember that there have always been times like these. The world has been through worse times. The United States has been through worse times. As the great American poet Robert Frost wrote, "In three words I can sum up everything I've learned about life: it goes on."[311]

---

309    Yuval Noah Harari, *Sapiens: A Brief History of Humankind* (New York: Harper Collins, 2015), p. 283.

310    O'Sullivan, *The Levelling*, 49.

311    Robert Frost, quote, The Old and Wise Monk website. http://www.oldandwisemonk.com/2020/08/in-three-words-i-can-sum-up-everything.html.

And it will. The question for our generations is what can we do to make progress so that life doesn't just go on but gets better. That is the subject we will address in the next chapter.

# CHAPTER 12

★ ★ ★ ★ ★ ★ ★

# IT'S NOT SIMPLE

My first few months of practice as a neurosurgeon were tense. After eighteen years of college, medical school, and residency, I signed on with a medium-sized hospital to start a new neurosurgical group. I did not know anyone in the community and early on felt alone and scared at times. In the process of recruiting others to join me, the existing group of neurosurgeons at the hospital left to work at a competing hospital down the street. The physicians, nurses, and technicians remaining at my hospital now had no other choice but to work closely with me and my group. Some embraced the change; others did not. But I was young, ambitious, and a bit naive. I believed we were capable of building a great neurosurgical team, but it was going to take the buy-in from other physicians, nurses, and technicians in the hospital to make it work. I kept two running mental lists, who was with us and who was not. I let those mental lists guide my behavior as to whom I trusted and who I kept at arm's length.

A better, more experienced, and secure version of myself would have realized the futility of keeping two lists. The physicians, nurses, and technicians at my hospital could not be divided into good and evil, trustworthy and untrustworthy. Each of them was a complex, thinking human being who had complex, conflicting thoughts about me and my group—some good, some bad. What my brain was doing in those early months of practice was taking a complex situation and trying to make it simple. I was dividing the world in two, which made the situation easier for me to manage.

Dividing the world into groups of two is deeply wired in each of us. Fundamental concepts like good and evil, male and female, friend and foe, wise and foolish, or rich and poor are labels that we unconsciously use to quickly group similar things. Doing so helps simplify the world around us. But just because we want the world to break down in a binary fashion doesn't mean it will bend to our will. In almost all cases in the natural world, there is a continuum, degrees of one versus another. An individual can be both one thing and its opposite at the same time. Beethoven brilliantly wrote the Ninth Symphony, but would carelessly lose his house keys.[312] Sir Isaac Newton was one of the greatest mathematicians in history but nearly went bankrupt over-speculating in the London stock market.[313]

The reality is that our world is complicated and complex and becomes more of both each day. There is a difference between complicated and complex problems. Complicated problems can be hard to solve, but nonetheless, are still solvable. Rules, recipes, and algorithms can be

---

312    Richard Thaler and Cass R. Sunstein, *Nudge: Improving Decisions about Health, Wealth, and Happiness* (New Haven, CT: Yale University Press, 2008), p. 19.

313    Thomas Levenson, "Investors Have Been Making the Same Mistake for 300 Years," *The Atlantic*, August 23, 2020. https://www.theatlantic.com/ideas/archive/2020/08/even-geniuses-make-bad-investors/615592/.

created that offer solutions to complicated problems. They can also be resolved with systems and processes, like the hierarchical structure that most companies use to command and control employees. Complex problems are different. Complex problems involve too many unknowns and interrelated factors to be solved with rules and processes. There is no algorithm for how to respond to a complex problem. Complex problem solving requires nimble, flexible thinking about the problem itself and any possible solutions. Solutions to complex problems come from a trial and error, iterative process that is continually refined, over and over again, indefinitely if necessary. Complex problem solving is an ongoing process that is indifferent to individual preferences, ideology, history, or long-held beliefs. Forecasting the weather for tomorrow is complicated. Forecasting the weather for next month is complex. Operating on a malignant brain tumor is complicated. Curing a patient of a malignant brain tumor is complex. Sending satellites into space to monitor climate change is complicated. Understanding and manipulating climate change is complex.

One of the foundations of conservative ideology is that social problems are complex, and thus, a single legislative solution to those problems, born from the intentionally slow process of deliberation and compromise, is going to be wrong almost every time. The results of programs that purport to tackle complex social problems never flow from their initial design; they are merely the result of swarms of independent variables that defy prediction and subordination.[314] For example, since the beginning of the government's war on poverty in the 1960s until today, the poverty rate in the U.S. has gone from 14.7 percent to 14.5 percent.[315] Not a remarkable improvement, but here is a sobering reality. During that

---

314    Will, *The Conservative Sensibility*, 349.

315    Brooks, *The Conservative Heart*, 62.

same time, the U.S. government has spent $23 trillion fighting poverty, and each year adds another $1 trillion toward the same goal, enough to give $21,000 to every person below the poverty line (much of the money ends up going to people above the poverty line).[316] Despite that heavy spending, the poverty rate remains essentially unchanged. The underlying problem is that government bureaucrats treat poverty like a complicated problem with a set of solutions instead of a complex problem laden with chaos and randomness that defies formulaic solutions. "The great strength of political conservatives at this time is that they are open to the thought that matters are complex. Liberals have got into a reflexive pattern of denying this," observed former New York Democratic senator Patrick Moynihan.[317]

Senator Moynihan was a brilliant politician and a keen student of history. Just over 160 years ago, Charles Darwin's fundamental insight was that species change by natural selection but do not do so to a predictable trajectory or to a predetermined end. Change occurs over time in response to local conditions, which themselves change over time. Liberals stick to their heartfelt belief that by using government power to change social conditions, predetermined social ends can be achieved. This is the type of simplistic thinking that led to liberals' support of eugenics—the controlled selective breeding of human populations—in the early twentieth century.[318]

A more realistic view of poverty is that the political and biological systems that lead to poverty are immensely complex. Factors such as geography,

---

316    Tanner, *The Inclusive Economy*, 10.

317    Joe Klein, "Daniel Patrick Moynihan Was Often Right", *New York Times*, May 24, 2021. https://www.nytimes.com/2021/05/15/books/review/daniel-patrick-moynihan-was-often-right-joe-klein-on-why-it-still-matters.html.

318    Will, *The Conservative Sensibility*, 51.

regional conflicts, healthcare, sanitation, clean water, weather patterns, education, infrastructure, and the strength of the local economy combine in chaotic, unpredictable ways to create the environment for poverty and wealth.[319] No federal government could possibly legislate an anti-poverty program to account for such complexity, nor could a legislative body be nimble enough to respond to the inevitable changes that occur with each of those factors over time. Within the boundaries of government bureaucracy, the best-case scenario for addressing complex social problems like poverty is to offer funding and broad autonomy to local governments in order to respond and adjust to the unique, ever-changing factors of their environment.

The complexity within social problems are daunting. Complexity makes us feel small and ineffective; thus, we persist in harboring a latent bias towards simplicity. Political extremism exploits that bias by perpetuating a notion that there is a right way of thinking, and anyone who dares to think otherwise is immoral, stupid, arrogant, or contemptuous. A fear of complexity draws us toward anyone peddling a simple solution, particularly if that alternative also has a clear and definable enemy. The addition of an enemy satisfies an irresistible urge to blame someone. Once the bad actors are identified, we give ourselves permission to simplify our thinking and blame those who don't think as we do for the outcome.

Listening to the one-sided debates on college campuses today makes it obvious that our youngest generation has been taught this strategy well. Video of these incidents shows young people who appear convinced that life is a battle between good and evil. It's a battle that brings out the loudest vitriol that does nothing but move us further away from

---

319    "11 Top Causes of Global Poverty," Concern Worldwide U.S., March 4, 2020. https://www.concernusa.org/story/causes-of-poverty/.

thoughtful dialog. Such one-sided shouting matches are anathema to progress. Political solutions to complex social problems in a democracy are, by design, a slow, grinding result of compromise. Social problems rarely have villains, and political solutions rarely have heroes.

The desire to find simple solutions and punish bad actors while ignoring the complexity of underlying social problems is prominently on display in the U.S. prison system. There are now three times more people with serious mental illnesses incarcerated in the United States than in hospitals. Of the 1,270,000 inmates in state prisons,[320] 73 percent of women and 55 percent of men have at least one mental health problem.[321] Remarkably, the United States incarcerates roughly 2.2 million prisoners in federal, state, and local jails. This is just under the 2.4 million prisoners in China and Russia combined.[322]

Incarceration serves as a default to deal with many of the biggest, most complex social problems facing our country. Incarceration doesn't solve those problems as much as it temporarily buries them. People who are homeless, unemployed, addicted, hungry, illiterate, or mentally ill can suddenly disappear into the prison system, making them possible to ignore. Their problems don't disappear, just the people.

Ninety-five percent of prisoners are released back into society. That's when their real problems begin. What is a former prisoner supposed to do when they get out? The most likely path is that they become

---

320    Wikipedia, "Incarceration in the United States," last accessed March 14, 2019, https://en.wikipedia.org/wiki/Incarceration_in_the_United_States.

321    Sarah Varney, "By the Numbers: Mental Illness behind Bars," SPBS News Hour, May 15, 2014. https://www.pbs.org/newshour/health/numbers-mental-illness-behind-bars.

322    "World Prison Populations," BBC, accessed March 13, 2019. http://news.bbc.co.uk/2/shared/spl/hi/uk/06/prisons/html/nn2page1.stm.

more isolated and alienated than when they went into prison. Not surprisingly, more than 40 percent of ex-convicts are back in prison within three years, and two-thirds are rearrested.[323] When the judicial system makes a criminal disappear into the prison system, we deter the harm they may cause for a while, but it doesn't rehabilitate them, and it doesn't keep us safe in the long run.

In addition, the consequences of incarceration don't end with the generation currently in prison. Boys whose parents are incarcerated are five times more likely to also be incarcerated. Those boys are more likely to go to prison than graduate from high school.[324] Crime and incarceration is an extremely complex social problem that has outstripped the simple solution of temporarily removing people from society.

Despite evidence surrounding us of the failure of simple solutions to complex social problems, we continually implement them. Simple solutions coming from ideological extremists are like intellectual gravity. The problem for anyone paying close attention is that the arguments made to implement simple solutions degenerates into an insistence upon ignorance. People who fancy themselves to be intellectually enlightened and certain of their understanding live in the clean, well-lit prison of one idea. Critical race theory is such a prison. It is born from an idea that the nature of everything, from political acts to intellectual works, is determined by race. Any simple idea purporting to explain something complex requires its adherents to be equally simple—not smart, able-minded people capable of working through complex problems over time with sophisticated, nuanced thought.[325]

---

323   Brooks, *The Conservative Heart*, 89.

324   Maya Schenwar, *Locked Down, Locked Out: Why Prison Doesn't Work and How We Can Do Better* (San Francisco, CA: Berrett-Kohler, 2014), p. 45.

325   Will, *The Conservative Sensibility*, 371.

To move toward that type of complex thought is an uphill battle. The more we learn, the more there is to know, and the smaller the share of all knowledge that any one mind can absorb. The more civilized we become, the more relatively ignorant any individual must become of the facts on which a working civilization depends.[326] In a way, ignorance really is bliss. We can fly without knowing how an airplane works. We can pick up our mobile phone without understanding anything about how digital clouds, electromagnetic fields, ultra-high frequency radio waves, and billions of silicon switches work together in order to text your best friend. The paradox of technology is that it offers more knowledge and dumbs us down at the same time. It makes simple solutions seem like they are common and even expected.

The more we ignore complexity, the more simple our thinking becomes, the more polarized our culture gets, and the more hate we have for "them". But within the complexity is where true understanding comes from. Diving into the complexity from opposite ends and meeting somewhere in the middle has been the quintessential method of democratic politics for 2,500 years. For example, conservatives place great value on the moral capital within a culture. Moral capital includes the values, virtues, and beliefs that enable communities to suppress selfishness and make cooperation possible. For liberals, moral capital is a blind spot. While they desire the same suppression of selfishness and cooperation essential for a functioning and just culture, they find moral capital too difficult to define and replicate over time. It is why liberal reforms often backfire and communist revolutions end in despotism. For conservatives, their blind spot is that they often fail to take notice of certain classes of victims, fail to limit powerful interests, and fail to see the need to change until it's too late. In order to have social cohesion,

---

326    Will, *The Conservative Sensibility*, 243.

there must be at least some recognition of our respective blind spots to find some overlap. Remaining at simplistic, ideological extremes results in no overlap, only a constant struggle of either being too ossified by tradition or too individualistic to cooperate and create the potential for progress.[327]

The debates that need to happen between liberals and conservatives are difficult. At times, some deliberately adopt simplified misrepresentations of what the opposition is saying in order to avoid the difficult conversation.[328] There is no better example of that avoidance than in the U.S. Congress. The U.S. House and Senate struggle to reach bipartisan consensus on nearly everything, and over the past sixty years have increasingly voted along party lines.[329] In 2015, 75 percent of House votes and 69 percent of Senate votes were along strict party lines.[330] In seventeen out of the last forty-six years, the fiscal year has started with zero completed appropriations bills. Over that near half century, Congress passed all its appropriations bills on time on only four occasions.[331] Small, gerrymandered districts of a like-minded population create a pool of voters that elect the most politically extreme congressional members to the House. Thus, House polarization is organic. The Senate is polarized for entirely different reasons. In the Senate, legislation grinds to a halt for

---

327    Haidt, *The Righteous Mind*, 342.

328    Murray, *The Madness of Crowds*, loc. 1425.

329    Akhil Jalan, "Political Partisanship: A look at the data," towards data science, August 2, 2017. https://towardsdatascience.com/political-partisanship-a-look-at-the-data-e71946199586.

330    "Party Unity Votes in Congress, 1953–2016," Vitalstats. https://www.brookings.edu/wp-content/uploads/2017/01/vitalstats_ch8_tbl3.pdf.

331    Leonard E. Burman, "It's Not News That Congress's Budget Process Is a Wreck, but It Should Be," Tax Policy Center, October 9, 2020. https://www.taxpolicycenter.org/taxvox/its-not-news-congresss-budget-process-wreck-it-should-be.

procedural reasons. Senate legislation overrides House-passed legislation totally or partially 82 percent of the time, and the Senate has the final say on all treaties and federal court nominations, including the Supreme Court.[332] Will Rogers has been dead for over eighty-five years, but his oft-repeated joke about Congress has never been more timely, "If pro is the opposite of con, what is the opposite of Congress?"[333]

The Senate tradition of unlimited debate allows for the use of the filibuster, a loosely defined term describing an action that will prolong debate and delay or prevent a vote. Prior to 1917, Senate rules did not offer a way to end debate and force a vote on a measure. That year, senators adopted a rule to allow a two-thirds majority to end a filibuster, a procedure known as "cloture." In 1975, the Senate reduced the number of votes required for cloture from two-thirds to three-fifths of all senators or sixty of the 100-member Senate.[334] If Senate leaders know that at least forty-one senators plan to oppose a cloture motion, they often choose not to even schedule the bill for floor consideration.[335]

In 1970, another procedural change in the Senate was created allowing the Senate to set aside a filibustered bill and move onto other matters with either the unanimous consent of the entire Senate or through the consent of the minority leader. Effectively, this made filibustering

---

332    Kristin Eberhard, "The Filibuster Stops Progress on Solutions Most Americans Want," Sightline Institute, April 26, 2021. https://tinyurl.com/2kwzauuh.

333    Will Rogers, quote, Goodreads.com. https://www.goodreads.com/quotes/323502-if-pro-is-the-opposite-of-con-what-is-the.

334    "About Filibusters and Cloture," U.S. Senate website. https://www.senate.gov/about/powers-procedures/filibusters-cloture.htm.

335    Molly E. Reynolds, "What is the Senate filibuster, and what would it take to eliminate it?" Polisy 2020, Brookings, September 9, 2020. https://www.brookings.edu/policy2020/votervital/what-is-the-senate-filibuster-and-what-would-it-take-to-eliminate-it/.

even easier.[336] From 1917 until 1970, there were only fifty-eight cloture motions filed. Since 1970, almost 2,000 have been filed because of the ease in doing so.[337] Now, even the threat of a filibuster is enough to kill a bill in the Senate. Moreover, when the Senate is dysfunctional, the House of Representatives might as well be because the bills House members send to the Senate go there to die.

The stalemate of inactivity in Congress concentrates power in the executive branch. Executive branch bureaucrats can make policy and rules without the debate and compromise inherent in the legislative branch. Executive branch bureaucrats are specialists, while legislators are generalists. Legislators spend only one-third of their time on policy making and legislative oversight. The remaining two-thirds of their time is given to constituent issues, communication, traveling, and campaigning for the next election. Congress is in session Tuesday through Thursday for one-third of the year, but the executive branch grinds on 365 days a year.

If Congress does finally pass a law, it is usually with minimal specificity due to an inability to find sufficient common ground. Minimizing the details avoids diving into the complexity. As such, the executive branch is charged with filling in the rules and regulations that congressionally passed bills avoid. Congress's complexity avoidance combined with federal courts that are deferential to Congress—avoiding broad interpretation and not asking that Congress write what it intends—means any distinction between the functions of the executive and legislative branch is effectively erased. Deferential courts have de facto sanctioned the growth of the executive branch and the administrative state.

---

336    "Filibuster in the United States Senate," Wikipedia. https://en.wikipedia.org/wiki/Filibuster_in_the_United_States_Senate.

337    Will, *The Conservative Sensibility*, 37.

Congress ignores complexity in the same way the rest of us do. Congress doesn't need to immerse itself in the details of legislation when the executive branch is there to take care of the details and make it work. While the legislative branch turns away from complexity, the executive branch has no choice but to embrace it. Embracing the complexity means considering more options and responding to changes and feedback quickly. It is more than any federal government, no matter how big or compassionate, can handle effectively.

Many conservatives believe that the answer to increasing complexity is to leave hard decisions to individuals, not government. The underlying doctrine for that belief being that rational people will make choices that are in their best interest or, at the very least, make choices that are better than if they were made by someone else.[338] Although attractive in theory, real-life experience fails to back up that belief. To see evidence to the contrary, put up an experienced chess player against a novice. The novice will lose because of inferior choices—choices that could be improved by some helpful hints. Many ordinary consumers make poor choices because they are interacting in a world inhabited by professional salesmen trying to sell them things. People tend to make good decisions when they have experience, good information, and prompt feedback. For example, it's easy for us to choose what flavor of ice cream we like, but it is harder to choose fruit over ice cream because the consequences of that decision are felt far into the future and the feedback is slow.

The Digital Revolution has connected us, given us access to more information, and teases with the notion that more information will lead to better choices. But more choices also makes for easy distractions. As Nobel laureate economist Herbert A. Simon puts it, "A wealth

---

338    Thaler and Sunstein, *Nudge*, 9.

of information creates a poverty of attention."[339] In such an era, the Libertarian notion of leaving every meaningful decision to the market is naive. Our reality is too complex for every individual to consistently make decisions that maximize their well-being on every issue. It is also too complex for any government to control.

A thoughtful conservative government focuses on issues that the private sector either can't or won't address. It targets programs that lie in the "middle ground" of human needs. A thoughtful conservative government knows it can't effectively provide food, clothing, and shelter for every citizen indefinitely. It must rely on individual families, charity, religious organizations, and local government to address community needs that are basic and essential. It also stays away from higher-level needs like meaningful relationships, self-esteem, and prestige, which are too personal and complex to solve.

A thoughtful conservative government stays in the middle ground of health, safety, and security. It maintains a defense on a national and local level that is capable of deterring or eliminating foreign and domestic terrorists, criminals, and radicals who are intent on bringing harm to its citizens. It monitors the economy, keeps trade flowing, and helps protect its businesses from having their intellectual property stolen in foreign markets. It helps care for people when they are too sick, disabled, or too feeble to care for themselves. It makes investments in its future by helping to educate young people. But it can't fix every complex social problem. It cannot rid a country of poverty, addiction, racism, sexism, or climate change. These are immensely complex social and environmental problems that no government is nimble enough to address.

---

339    Hal R. Varian, "The Information Economy: How much will two bits be worth in the digital marketplace?" https://people.ischool.berkeley.edu/~hal/pages/sciam.html.

That's not to say that a thoughtful conservative government shouldn't aspire to be nimble. A government that becomes too ossified to try anything new is in a countdown to its end. A thoughtful conservative government experiments with different types of prison reform; it doesn't just build more prisons. It tries different types of immigration reform that bring in skilled as well as unskilled workers rather than just opening the border or building a wall.

Thinking nimbly and being disciplined at the same time is difficult, but is a way of nibbling away at complex problems. It is a means of working in a scientific way from complexity to complicated to simple. "Taking something simple and making it complicated is common. Taking something that is complicated and making it simple is creativity," observed composer Charles Mingus.

The road is long. "For the simplicity that lies on this side of complexity, I would not give a fig. But for the simplicity that lies on the other side of complexity, I would give my life," said former Supreme Court justice Oliver Wendell Holmes. In this era, we need bold leaders and politicians capable of differentiating the complicated from the complex, to focus on what is possible and steer away from what is too complex. That type of thinking can start us on a path to keep our country together and make progress for generations to come. What must follow from that starting point is the subject of the next chapter.

# CHAPTER 13

★ ★ ★ ★ ★ ★ ★

# FACTS AND PROBLEMS

For some conservatives, times have never been worse. New York Times writer David Brooks observes, "Since the (2020 presidential) election, large swaths of the Trumpian right have decided America is facing a crisis like never before, and they are the small army of warriors fighting with Alamo-level desperation to ensure the survival of the country as they conceive it."[340]

If you're amongst the conservatives who have chosen to feel the way Mr. Brooks describes, I understand. The last twelve chapters of this book have made the case for substantiating those feelings. But if your mind is open to taking a break from dark thoughts and objectively looking at this moment in history from a slightly different perspective, there

---

340    David Brooks, "The GOP is getting worse," *Arkansas Democrat Gazette*, April 25, 2021. https://www.arkansasonline.com/news/2021/apr/25/the-gop-is-getting-worse/?opinion.

are alternatives to waking up tomorrow and embracing "Alamo-level desperation."

A thoughtful conservative that accepts the complexity of the problems facing our country is also capable of distinguishing between facts and problems. Facts are things that have already occurred or do not have an alternative. Facts don't change in response to anyone's feelings, they just *are*. Facts can be given context and meaning, but they can't be changed. As former senator Daniel Patrick Moynihan famously said, "Everyone is entitled to his own opinion, but not his own facts."[341] Problems, on the other hand, are unsettled questions. Problems are surrounded by doubt and uncertainty and can change in response to the feelings they generate. Potential solutions to problems lead to very different futures. Soviet Union Air Defense Force lieutenant, Stanislav Petrov was working an overnight shift in September 1983 when he faced a problem with history-changing consequences. Petrov's computer showed five U.S. missiles inbound for the Soviet Union. One option for Petrov was to follow orders and inform his superior officers. Those officers almost certainly would have followed their own orders and taken the next steps toward launching a counter strike, ending the world as we know it. Another option was to pause and double-check his computer. Thankfully for all of us, Petrov double-checked, realized that it was a malfunction, and prevented a nuclear holocaust.[342]

Far too often, we conflate facts and problems. A house that has burned to the ground is a fact. Figuring out what caused the fire is a problem. A single house that has burned to the ground must be investigated and the

---

341    Wikipedia, "Daniel Patrick Moynihan." https://tinyurl.com/f45ak5mh.

342    Pavel Aksenov, "Stanislav Petrov: The man who may have saved the world," BBC News, September 26, 2013. https://www.bbc.com/news/world-europe-24280831.

cause of the fire determined to give the incident context and meaning in order to make an appropriate response. For example, what if there were similar fires in the same area? If so, a local investigation to determine if there was a pattern of timing, accelerants, burn patterns, or tampered utilities would be appropriate. What if the wiring in the house was at fault and all homes built across the country around the same time had the same type of wiring? That would be a huge problem and appropriately generate a nation-wide response. But what if the smoke alarm in the burned-down home didn't have a battery? Would it be logical to believe that other houses in the neighborhood had the same problem? Would it mean that all other houses in the same city had the same problem? The entire country? What has happened in the past doesn't prophesy the composition and scope of problems in the future. Facts determine *if* there is a problem and the scope of that problem. Applying the same logic in reverse by assuming the cause and scope of the problem and searching for facts to justify the problem is nonsensical.

An analogy can be made to complex social problems like police misconduct. In 2019, there were just over ten million arrests by police officers in the United States,[343] 2.67 million of those arrested were Black men.[344] The deaths of Black men who died during police arrests, such as George Floyd in Minnesota, Michael Brown in Missouri, and Eric Garner in New York, are facts that rightly focus our attention on police misconduct. It is also factual that nationwide, Black men are more likely

---

343    "Number of Arrests for All Offenses in the United States from 1990 to 2020," statista. https://www.statista.com/statistics/191261/number-of-arrests-for-all-offenses-in-the-us-since-1990/.

344    "Law Enforcement & Juvenile Crime," Statistical Briefing Book, US Department of Justice Office of Justice Programs. https://www.ojjdp.gov/ojstatbb/crime/ucr.asp?table_in=2.

to be arrested and killed by police than white men.[345] I would hope that every American, conservative or liberal, would never condone police misconduct of any type on anyone regardless of race. Moreover, I would hope that every American would want to see involved police officers brought to justice and the victims' families compensated. But does the fact that George Floyd was killed while being arrested by members of the Minneapolis police 3rd Precinct mean that all police officers in the Minneapolis 3rd Precinct are guilty of misconduct or racism? Does it mean that the entire police force of Minneapolis is guilty of the same sins and character flaws? How about the police forces all across Minnesota? In the entire United States? And while we would all love to see any future acts of police misconduct or racism prevented, does anyone seriously believe that every applicant with a racist heart or a brutish demeanor wishing to join a police force can be reliably identified and culled out? Doing so would be the equivalent of fireproofing every house in every neighborhood in America—good in theory but impossible to implement.

Commingling facts and problems reveals a basic asymmetry to life. The most positive events of our lives are preceded by difficulty and take time to unfold. Negative events happen with ease and take less time. Building a house takes a long time. Burning it down is quick. Building a personal reputation takes a lifetime. Losing a reputation can take five seconds. Front page news is generally bad news, while steady progress isn't even newsworthy. Optimism is the best bet for most people because the world tends to get better over time, but pessimism is more common and

---

345    Lynne Peeples, "What the data says about police brutality and racial bias and which reforms might work," *nature*, June 19, 2020. https://www.nature.com/articles/d41586-020-01846-z.

sounds smarter.[346] The psychological tendency for everyone, including journalists and pundits that influence national conversations, is to focus on bad news. That tendency leads us to believe this moment in history is worse than it really is, and more importantly, that the future is likely to be even worse than it is now.[347] "For reasons I have never understood, people like to hear that the world is going to hell,"[348] observed historian Deirdre McCloskey.

Similarly, most of the people that influence our perspective—family, friends, media-types, cultural, business, and political leaders—have plenty of cautionary advice to offer, but rarely is there a penalty when they give the wrong advice. Their pessimism may be on point in the short term, but over the long term it is consistently wrong. A line drawn through the peaks and valleys of the centuries always has an upward trend, no matter how smart advice to the contrary sounds.

Still, when the perception of crisis and revolution arises, there are those that pine for the past. They desire a return to mythical times gone by when life was easier, men were stronger, women were prettier, and the family dog never peed on the carpet. Their desire is doomed to failure. As the famous engineer and industrialist Charles Kettering said, "You can't have a better tomorrow if you're thinking about yesterday."[349] That sentiment is particularly true if yesterday wasn't as good as you remember it to be. The cycle of the generations is inevitable, and the

---

346    Morgan Housel, *The Psychology of Money: Timeless Lessons on Wealth, Greed, and Happiness* (Petersfield, United Kingdom: Harriman House, 2020), loc. 1793, Kindle.

347    Bailey and Tupy, *Ten Global Trends*, 2.

348    Housel, *The Psychology of Money*, loc. 1793.

349    Charles Franklin Kettering, "Prophet of progress: selections from the speeches of Charles F. Kettering", 1961.

past does not return. It is inherent that the next generation moves in the opposite direction of the one before. Perhaps because the next generation forms values in their youth when thinking is more black and white, they are seemingly incapable of finding a middle ground. This is not just the case for U.S. culture. It has been true for all of recorded history. An inscription on the tablets of Babylonian clay dating back to 1000 BC when translated reads, "Today's youth is rotten, evil, godless and lazy. It will never be what youth used to be, and it will never be able to preserve our culture."[350] There are similar complaints in all cultures in all time periods.

Many millennials and Gen Z'ers rail against the America they see and long for a less capitalist, more socialist government.[351] But capitalism, by its very nature, has always generated wealth and envy. Envy can consume those who define their happiness relative to those around them. Karl Marx identified the social instability that accompanies capitalism.[352] It is its first and most palpable defect. The cycle of profit, speculation, irrational exuberance, stock market panic, and recession has been an endemic feature since the Industrial Revolution. The creative destruction of capitalism always has a price. That price is insecurity.

But for those same young adults that see socialism as the only other option to a conservative agenda that is too ossified to create change for the better, take heart. Today, even the most conservative political

---

350    Robert Greene, *The Laws of Human Nature* (New York: Penguin Random House, 2018), p. 541.

351    Hillary Hoffower, "70% of millennials say they'd vote for socialist. 5 facts about their debt-saddled economic situation tell you why," Insider, November 1, 2019. https://www.businessinsider.com/millennials-would-vote-socialist-bernie-sanders-elizabeth-warren-debt-2019-10.

352    John Plender, *Capitalism: Money, Morals, and the Markets* (London, UK: Biteback Publishing, 2015), loc. 36, Kindle.

movements promise change or reform of some sort. No politician, conservative or liberal, no matter how charming, could get elected by running on a platform of staying the same. The root word for *conservative* is the Latin term *conservare*, which means to preserve or keep intact. No thoughtful conservative I know wants to preserve everything. No one wants to preserve sexism or racism. No one wants to preserve economic classism or political dynasties. Thoughtful conservatives want to conserve some of the principles on which our country was founded but not everything. Thoughtful conservatives want to conserve liberty, free speech, freedom of religion, due process of law, and freedom of assembly-not slavery or misogyny. Thoughtful conservatives think in degrees, not all-or-nothing. Longing for their countrymen to value the rights fashioned in the Constitution and defended by the generations of Americans who have come before us is not akin to wishing the days of slavery would return. With the decline of religion in the United States, the Constitution may be the only thing that continues to bind us together. Thoughtful conservatives can look at the values embodied by the Founding Fathers and desire to preserve those that are core to the American success story while letting go of values that we now rightfully revile.

Conservatives have not always helped themselves in making distinctions of degree. Conservatives have stoked a fear in liberals over the past decade that anyone who labels themselves a conservative is opposed to change and innovation. Whatever liberals endorse, conservatives reject. It is a fear that prevents liberals who might be curious and want to engage in meaningful dialog about *how* to change. Instead, there is no dialog, and the only issue on the table is *if* there should be change. The cure for fear has always been engagement, exchange, and open-mindedness. Overcoming the fear of one another takes time, a thoughtful review of the evidence, and engagement with liberals and conservatives who share a similar curiosity and desire to improve.

From a thoughtful conservative perspective, now is not the time for Alamo-level desperation. Much of the social change we are witnessing in the early twenty-first century is not unexpected and not all bad. Throughout history, social values change with income. As families, cultures, and countries become wealthier, they are less concerned about security and more concerned about freedom. With nearly 90 percent of Americans living above the poverty level,[353] less time spent working,[354] and just over 35 percent with a college education,[355] it is not surprising that more people than ever before are feeling the empowerment to express their opinion and have raised their expectations for how they, their family, friends, and neighbors should be treated.

More discretionary income, less time spent working, and a higher level of education have also resulted in a rearrangement of America's national priorities. The basic physiologic and safety needs that a poor country must prioritize have been supplanted by psychological and self-fulfillment needs, such as meaningful relationships, feelings of accomplishment, and the expression of creativity. Insisting that racism and sexism end and that all Americans have the opportunity to live their best life is a rational consequence of wanting to create a culture consistent with those priorities.

Expressing those priorities has become exceedingly easy with social media. Social media may be a waste of time for many and is a treasure

---

353    "Poverty Rates in the United States from 1990 to 2020," statista. https:// www.statista.com/statistics/200463/us-poverty-rate-since-1990/.

354    Bailey and Tupy, *Ten Global Trends*, 92.

355    "Percentage of the U.S. population who have completed four years of college or more 1940 to 2020, by gender," statista. https://tinyurl.com/7t8eh6w5.

trove for corporations that profit from users' data, but it's also a remarkably efficient way to share our ideas. Widespread communication of new priorities naturally causes a reaction by those who wish for priorities to remain the same, but pushback against social change has always occurred. Pundits in the golden era of American culture from the 1890s through the 1950s deplored the trends of that time, just as much as hard-core conservatives do today.[356] Nostalgia is misplaced, and the good ol' days never return, but Alamo-level desperation doesn't pave the way to a better future either.[357] Cultural change has and will continue to occur no matter how much anyone wants the past to carry over into the future.

Alamo-level desperation is not unusual amongst those that feel strongest about resisting change. Regardless of political ideology, Americans tend to overreact to crises. That overreaction has often made our country better in an enduring way. Pearl Harbor resulted in the creation of the greatest navy the world has ever seen. Deployment of the Russian satellite Sputnik resulted in an overhaul of our education and research priorities to help create the greatest explosion of space and telecommunications technology in history. The oil crisis of the late 1970s resulted in more advanced deep-water and shale oil exploration, which has changed the course of history.

Although the entire story has yet to play out, the same overreaction can be seen in Americans' responses to the COVID-19 pandemic. Before the COVID-19 pandemic, getting a new vaccine from concept

---

356    Edward Tenner, *The Efficiency Paradox: What Big Data Can't Do* (New York: Penguin Random House, 2018) p. 85.

357    Tenner, *The Efficiency Paradox*, 86.

to approval could take ten years and billions of dollars.[358] Remarkably, it was only nine months between the World Health Organization's (WHO) declaration of the COVID-19 global pandemic and the Food and Drug Administration's (FDA) approval for the Pfizer/BioNTech mRNA vaccine for emergency use. Four days after the FDA's approval, healthcare workers were being vaccinated, and five months later, half of all Americans were vaccinated.[359] No other country of similar size has come close to that kind of response.

If historical facts like those still don't persuade you away from Alamo-level desperation, perhaps a thoughtful view of the future might. Despite the complex social problems facing Americans and the hatred we currently have for one another, there is no other country in the world better situated to thrive for the next several generations. A nation needs four primary assets to sustain itself over time: usable lands with defensible borders, a reliable food supply, a sustainable population structure, and access to a stable mixture of energy inputs.[360] More than any other country in the world, the United States has been blessed with those assets in abundance. Two oceans on the east and west, a desert to the south, and heavily forested areas to the north provide defensible borders around some of the most productive farmland in the world. Although the rate of population growth has slowed in the past twenty years, the U.S. population sits at around 330 million, increased by 10 percent between 2000 and 2010, and is projected to increase by 8

---

358    Alison Caldwell, "How were researches able to develop COVID-19 vaccines so quickly?" UChicago News, February 5, 2021. https://news.uchicago.edu/story/how-were-researchers-able-develop-covid-19-vaccines-so-quickly.

359    Bill Chappell, "Half of All U.S. Adults Are Now Fully Vaccinated against COVID-19," NPR.org, May 25, 2021. https://tinyurl.com/2bbhbv87.

360    Zeihan, *Disunited Nations,* loc. 1003.

percent between 2010 and 2020.[361] A large population gives the United States an economy of scale that is rare among the world's other 194 countries. The United States also possess some of the largest oil shale deposits in the world,[362] has the second largest output of wind generated electricity,[363] the second largest output of solar generated electricity,[364] and the fourth largest output of hydroelectric power.[365]

From a geographic, demographic, and resource perspective, the United States is in an ideal position to thrive in a world where nationalism is the prevailing theme and Americans no longer serve as the de facto police force for the world. Despite those remarkable assets, one of those necessary elements for national sustainability divides conservatives and liberals. While U.S. borders are geographically defensible, actually defending them, particularly on the southern border with Mexico, has become a political impasse. While both conservatives and liberals voice growing support for increasing legal immigration,[366] an open southern border and illegal immigration are extremely polarizing issues. Seventy-

---

361    Kevin Pollard, Linda A. Jacobsen, and Mark Matter, "The US Population Is Growing at the Slowest Rate Since the 1930s," PRB, February 8, 2020. https://www.prb.org/resources/u-s-population-growing-at-slowest-rate-since-the-1930s/.

362    "Shale Oil and Shale Gas are Globally Abundant," U.S.Energy Information Administration, January 2, 2014. https://www.eia.gov/todayinenergy/detail.php?id=14431.

363    Jack Unwin, "The top ten countries in the world by energy capacity," Power Technology, March 14, 2019. https://www.power-technology.com/features/wind-energy-by-country/.

364    "Solar Power by Country," World Population Review." https://worldpopulationreview.com/country-rankings/solar-power-by-country.

365    "Largest hydroelectric power generating countries worldwide in 2019," statista, https://tinyurl.com/msz57rbw.

366    "Shifting Public Views on Immigration into the U.S.," Pew Research Center, June 28, 2018. https://tinyurl.com/hujbs9z5.

eight percent of Republicans see open borders and illegal immigration as a critical threat, while only 19 percent of Democrats feel the same way.[367] Illegal immigration and an open southern border have become the bellwether issue as to whether Americans can continue to work out their political differences in constructive ways.

Like all social issues, illegal immigration and open borders are complex. America is a country of immigrants. Immigration has been a source of great strength for the United States as generation after generation of immigrants added their energy and skills to the workforce. Each generation of immigrants has also added to the complexity of American culture by bringing in their unique religion, beliefs, and values. Complex and diverse cultures are resilient. In nature, ecosystems without diversity are barren and fragile. When the forces of nature combine to destroy a monoculture, nothing remains. This is why during droughts, suburban bluegrass lawns that aren't cared for and watered become scorched and die. Conversely, livestock pastures in the same area, often populated with more than twenty different types of grasses, legumes, and forbs, survive by supporting each other. Legumes like clover and alfalfa take nitrogen from the air and release it from their root system to feed nearby grass plants with proteins. Forbs like milkweed or sunflowers send down deep roots that soak up moisture from the morning dew and prevent compaction of the soil during times of drought. The diverse polyculture of pasture plants finds ways to help each other survive the same forces of nature that kill off the suburban lawn monoculture only a few yards away.

---

367     Craig Kafura and Bettina Hammer, "Republicans and Democrats in Different Worlds on Immigration," The Chicago Council on Global Affairs, October 8, 2019. https://tinyurl.com/svdu6dh4.

Similarly, the healthiest and most celebrated human cultures throughout history have been ones in which internal diversity amongst individuals was encouraged and exploited. Ancient Athens, the Sung Dynasty, the Italian Renaissance, and the western world in the 1920s were richly diverse.[368] Contrast those with the conformity and cultural sterility of a Stalin or Hitler dictatorship.

It is not a coincidence that the United States is the home to so many immigrants. Democracy is the only form of government that can accommodate a large influx of immigrants. Democracies require negotiation, compromise, and concessions. Setbacks are inevitable, and victories are often partial. Democracy involves the type of grinding work that authoritarians despise.[369]

There is a loss of cultural sophistication in societies that do not grow by immigration and become cut off from the rest of the populace. This happened in Tasmania after the ice age 10,000 years ago, when Tasmanians were cut off from the rest of the world by rising waters. Over time, the Tasmanian people lost the ability to fish and were shocked by the presence of other human beings when Europeans landed there in the seventeenth century. In contrast, populations that grow by immigration accumulate culture more rapidly and learn to accommodate and adapt to changes in their environment.[370] "It is hardly possible to overstate the value in the present state of human improvement of placing human beings in contact with other people dissimilar to themselves and with modes of thought and action unlike those with which they are

---

368    Robert Greene, *The Laws of Human Nature* (New York: Penguin Random House, 2018), p. 374.

369    Levitsky and Ziblatt, *How Democracies Die*, 77.

370    Rutherford, *Humanimal,* 220.

familiar," said the famous nineteenth-century political economist John Stuart Mill.[371]

The history of the United States reveals a back and forth struggle with immigration. While the strengths of immigration have become obvious over time, there has always been fear about the cultural complexity created by an influx of immigrants. In his day, Thomas Jefferson fretted that a flood of immigrants would warp or bias the American direction and turn the culture into a heterogenous, incoherent, distracted mass.[372] Of course, that has not happened. Instead, immigrants to America tend to gravitate to a middle ground to become their own form of "similar but different." Native languages get mixed in with English. Customs, cuisine, holidays, and fashion morph into something that is authentic yet unique to an immigrant culture that gets blended in with many others.

Some far-right conservatives fear that the internationalization of culture from Starbucks to Star Wars will cause national borders to fall like in East and West Germany.[373] This is not a fear based on historical fact. Societies never freely merged together. They simply took things from other cultures, made them their own in some novel way, and moved on. The cultures of the indigenous Indians, Africans, and Portuguese merged together and formed the modern Brazilian way of life. The annual Portuguese-influenced Carnival in Rio de Janeiro is one of the best parties in the world. During Carnival, African samba music is played alongside indigenous Indian artwork. More than one-third of Londoners are foreign born, coming from 270 different countries and speaking over 300 different languages. The influx of immigrants has

---

371    Ian Leslie, *Curious: The Desire to Know and Why Your Future Depends on It* (New York, Basic Books, 2014) p. 65.

372    Moffett, *The Human Swarm*, 356.

373    Moffett, *The Human Swarm*, 378.

permanently changed the collective palate of Londoners, making curry houses more popular than fish and chip pubs.[374]

An invasion by space aliens threatening the future of the world would not make nations less relevant. Responding to such an attack, people of various nations might forget their nationality for a time and bond together to fight against a threat, but that would not negate the weight we place on our differences. The notion that the nations of the world could somehow come together under some cosmopolitan government is a pipe dream.[375]

Despite our complex social problems, the appeal of the United States for potential immigrants remains strong. Humans vote with their feet. Many want to move to the United States, Canada, Australia, or Germany. Perhaps a few want to move to China or Japan. Nobody wants to move to Russia where oligarchs rule with endemic corruption, malfunctioning services, no rule of law, and staggering inequality. Similarly, an oft-repeated conservative fear that global Islam could take over the world flies in the face of reality. A global Islamic caliphate may appeal to Syrians or the disenfranchised Muslim youth of Germany and France, but it is hard to imagine the disgruntled of Greece, Brazil, or South Africa aching to join such a cabal.[376]

It is not a single religion, race, or ethnicity that makes a culture, but rather it is the culture that determines the type of people capable of

---

374   "270 nationalities and 300 different languages: how a United Nations of workers is driving London forward," *Evening Standard,* April 12, 2012. https://tinyurl.com/4xesu7w8.

375   Moffett, *The Human Swarm,* 380.

376   Yuval Noah Harari, *21 Lessons for the 21st Century* (New York: Penguin Random House, 2018), p. 12.

thriving within it.[377] The defining problem for the United States today is whether a country with the largest immigrant population in the world, many complex social problems, widening income inequality, and a federal government with no limits to its scope can make choices that allow it to survive for another generation.[378] How its people should live—which human goals should be exalted—will not result in a single, universally satisfying answer. Thus, Americans must be prepared either for perpetual fighting or find a way to accommodate. Compromise is the oxygen of democracy. The lively sense liberals have of the possibility of progress is matched by a conservative sense of the possibility of decline. Both concerns need attending. A far-right, uncompromising posture with Alamo-type desperation by conservatives taunts liberals who are gaining numbers over time as the populations of liberal millennials and Gen Z grow and the more conservative baby boomer generation shrinks. In response to conservative's taunts, liberals might borrow the infamous Taliban line, "You have the watches, but we have the time."[379]

The engagement that must ensue between conservatives and liberals, particularly on important issues like immigration, are crucial. Conservatives cannot allow their views to be shouted down or marginalized. "Nothing lowers the level of conversation more than raising the voice," said poet Stanley Horowitz.[380] In a democracy, no human right is more important than free speech.[381] Without it, no other right

---

377    Durant, *The Lessons of History*, loc. 270.

378    Will, *The Conservative Sensibility*, 122.

379    Anthony Isola, "You Have the Watches, But We Have the Time," A Teachable Moment, September 8, 2015. https://tonyisola.com/2015/09/you-have-the-watches-but-we-have-the-time/.

380    Stanley Horowitz, Rajesh Setty, Quotes worth recording. https://rajeshsetty.com/2006/04/28/quotes-worth-recording-stanley-horowitz/.

381    Bailey and Tupy, *Ten Global Trends*, 51.

can be asserted or defended. It is the best means we have to find social, economic, political, and scientific truth. But far-right absolutists and authoritarian conservatives who cannot tolerate criticism of their views have little influence in such debates. In a negotiation where both parties can walk away from the table, hard-liners rarely get what they came for. When conversations carry more statements than questions, curiosity ends, thoughts become stagnant, and stalemate ensues. Cultures where people feel they can speak freely and be listened to flourish. Societies where speech is muzzled or opposing thoughts have no ears willing to hear them shrivel.[382] This is true regardless if the muzzling is done by an oppressive government or the unbridled authority of private companies that control the distribution of speech and language.

Thoughtful, constructive arguments, the back and forth between people with opposing ideas, contain the story of American progress in slow, unsteady steps over the arc of time. The sound of political speech in a democratic society is an uneven symphony that produces intolerable noise most of the time but occasionally is punctuated by the dazzling harmony that only comes from many instruments playing together. Harmonies don't emerge when one section overpowers the rest. Musicians who cannot play with the same loudness, pitch, contour, rhythm, and tempo as the rest of the symphony ruin the opportunity to create great music. But becoming a great musician is not accomplished by merely playing with the rest of the symphony. Great musicians are made in eons of lonely moments—studying and practicing on their own to perfect their craft.

Similarly, the citizens of a democracy are effective when they think for themselves and, in the words of Voltaire, give others the privilege to do

---

382    Bailey and Tupy, *Ten Global Trends*, 51.

so as well.[383] People who think for themselves, regardless of political ideology, are owners of their own destinies rather than pawns of the elite.[384] It is not the role of journalists, media personalities, politicians, leaders, or activists to think for everyone else. Journalists have to compete for our attention with exciting stories and dramatic narratives. They focus on the unusual as opposed to the common, the dramatically new rather than slowly changing patterns, the bad over gradual, steady improvement.[385]

Reflecting our reality is not something we can expect journalists or politicians to do. They give us snapshots based on their beliefs. Even the most neutral news organizations and non-dramatic politicians can't just report data without interpreting it for their audience. Data is overwhelmingly boring, but that is where the answers are. Having others interpret our world is just as misleading as ignoring data altogether.

Likewise, listening to advocates is equally misleading. Advocates are not experts, and the more someone wants a deeply held conviction to be true, the more likely they are to believe a story that overestimates the odds of it being true.[386] Advocates offer perspective, but like everyone else from journalists to politicians, pundits, family, and friends, they cannot think for you.

Thinking is hard work. It takes time. The American philosopher William James understood how hard thinking could be when he said, "A great

---

383   Voltaire, Treatise on Tolerance, 1763.

384   Heimans and Timms, *New Power,* 252.

385   Hans Rosling, *Factfulness: Ten Reasons We're Wrong About the World, and Why Things Are Better Than You Think* (New York: Flatiron, 2018), p. 210.

386   Morgan Housel, *The Psychology of Money: Timeless Lessons on Wealth, Greed, and Happiness* (Petersfield, United Kingdom: Harriman House, 2020), loc. 1988, Kindle.

many people think they are thinking when they are merely rearranging their prejudices."[387] Thinking citizens in a democracy are continually burdened by imagining they might be wrong. If you can't imagine you could be wrong, what's the point of thoughtful exchange with others? On a higher level, if you can't imagine being wrong, what's the point of living in a democracy? And if you can't imagine why or how others think differently, then how could you tolerate living in a democracy?[388]

The path of the thoughtful conservative is full of contradiction and disappointment. There are times when listening to liberal mantras is culturally incomprehensible. The first time I heard a speaker espouse the liberal belief that gender could be defined by how one feels and not by genetics, my mind went blank. I could not wrap my thoughts around such a concept. It was as if an attempt was being made to cast aside everything I had ever learned about genetics with one statement. My brain had no place for even considering such a concept. I stared back at the speaker in bewilderment, hopeless that there was any meaningful dialog to be had about something that sounded like pure nonsense. But as F. Scott Fitzgerald wrote, "The test of a first-rate intelligence is the ability to hold two opposing ideas in mind at the same time and still retain the ability to function. One should, for example, be able to see that things are hopeless yet be determined to make them otherwise."[389] Just because things appear hopeless now doesn't mean they will be for all time. The speaker had just used words to describe his views on the determination of gender. When the talk was over, what had been said became fact. It was up to me to determine if I now had a problem.

---

387   William James, *Forbes* Quotes. https://www.forbes.com/quotes/10021/.

388   Warren Berger, *A More Beautiful Question: The Power of Inquiry to Spark Breakthrough Ideas* (New York: Bloomsbury, 2014), loc. 985, Kindle.

389   "Giving Up Your Best Loved Ideas and Starting Over," Farnam Street media website, https://fs.blog/2014/12/dani-shapiro-still-writing/.

A thoughtful conservative that thinks for themselves and gives others the privilege to do so as well doesn't ascribe motives to others that are meaner than their own. Intentions matter. When we ascribe bad intentions to someone's actions, it becomes the lens we view all their actions through. Implying bad intentions can quickly lead to the belief that they are a bad person. More likely, their intentions are more complex than either good or bad. My own desire to see values such as liberty, free speech, and due process endure are born from a belief that the best of what human beings can become are revealed when nations embrace those values. It is not born from a desire to see racism thrive. By the same measure, I cannot assume that even a concept as foreign as defining sex by feelings is born from some evil vein running through liberal ideology. Surely, such a belief comes from a place of caring for other people and a desire to see the culture create a space to thrive for those who share such feelings.

Engaging in the critical arguments of our time is difficult, but it doesn't have to result in Alamo-type desperation. It also doesn't preclude you from being happy. As vocalist Gerald Way wrote, "Being happy doesn't mean everything is perfect. It means you have decided to look beyond the imperfections."[390] Democracies are imperfect governments composed of imperfect people. Imperfect but still capable of being thoughtful. It is time for a political reawakening. It is time for us to move beyond simple hard-line decrees and dogma. It is time to think for ourselves, distinguish fact from problem, and decide who we are and what we can be over the next decade. That is the subject of the final chapter.

---

390    "Everything MCR, Reddit. https://tinyurl.com/5x3nxauj.

# CHAPTER 14
★ ★ ★ ★ ★ ★ ★

# TIME FOR A POLITICAL REAWAKENING

If a far-right reviewer were to sum up the theme of this book in one sentence, it would likely include the words "moderate conservative." Today in most conservative circles, moderate is not a label viewed favorably. There are legitimate reasons. Moderate conservatives tend to use their moniker with a bit of moral grandstanding and the not-so-subtle implication that extremists are far too wicked to be trusted. Moderate can also be code for "tolerant," which many conservatives detest. But the primary knock on moderate conservatives by the far-right is that moderates dismiss extremists who dare to disagree with more mainstream views. In a Republican Party that deplores cancel culture, the far-right is particularly annoyed at attempts at being canceled by their own kind.

While I can't disagree with the first two criticisms, the far-right's interpretation of dismissal seems to get confused with disagreement. The difference between moderate and extreme is a matter of degree, not a matter of principle. While a hard-right conservative believes that hierarchy and inequality are part of the natural order of a capitalist system, is it so different for a moderate conservative to also believe that another part of the natural order is for the government to help care for those who can't care for themselves? The bedrock conservative belief that capitalism is the best economic system ever created doesn't mean that we also must be indifferent to the suffering of those living on the underside of capitalism's inequality. It's not that those who occupy the political middle ground are against free markets or capitalism; it's a question of managing the inevitable economic fallout from those systems. The consequence of the Republican Party's indifference to that fallout and its move to its partisan extreme is that it is losing its appeal to the general electorate and thus losing power. By electing far-right candidates in primaries, the Republican Party is becoming less appealing to voters in the general election.[391] If conservatives fail to throttle down on a rigid partisan platform and hatred toward liberals, we are taking ourselves down a dark path. In the words of Nelson Mandela, "When we dehumanize and demonize our opponent, we abandon the possibility of peacefully resolving our differences and seek to justify violence against them."[392] Up until the last transition of presidential power in the United States, I thought Mr. Mandela's sentiments applied to other countries and other political parties—not U.S. Republicans. I no longer hold that belief.

---

391  Andrew B. Hall, "What Happens When Extremists Win Primaries?" Cambridge University Press," March 3, 2015. https://tinyurl.com/yr2f3nkp.

392  Greg Lukianoff and Jonathan Haidt, *The Coddling of the American Mind: How Good Intentions and Bad Ideas Are Setting Up a Generation for Failure* (New York: Penguin, 2018), p. 81.

Thus far I have tried to make the case that Americans on the far-right and left political extremes have come to hate each other. There are reasons for that hatred: fear, inequality of power, racism, religious beliefs, media bias, and distrust of science, government, and business. People who feel the most hatred also tend to be the most politically active. The energy of their emotion compels them to speak out, write, protest, and advocate for their point of view. Those who feel more indifference than hatred, less faith, and more cynicism, are less politically active. Moderates invest less of their energy in politics. They don't get invited to political fundraisers, they watch less partisan cable news, and to the detriment of moderate authors, they buy fewer political books.

The truth is that most moderate Americans treat politics as a hobby. We read social media to satisfy emotional or expression needs.[393] Having conversation-capable political knowledge is akin to having a similar level of sports knowledge. It's entertaining and gives us enough information to engage in polite online banter and chat around the water cooler. Most of us are not looking to become political advocates or alter the outcome of an election. We are merely looking for credible information that confirms our own political views and candidates that, while we might not agree with some of their positions, are thoughtful and reasonable.

Moderates, regardless of political affiliation, are typically less devout in their political beliefs compared to partisans and avoid political conversations because they find them to be too divisive.[394] Nearly everyone who treats politics as more than just a hobby—predominantly those at the political extreme—reports engaging in politics as a duty

---

393     Eitan Hersch, *Politics Is for Power:* How to Move Beyond Political Hobbyism, Take Action, and Make Real Change (New York: Simon & Schuster, 2020), p. 10.

394     Molly Ball, "Moderates: Who Are They and What Do They Want?", *The Atlantic*, May 15, 2014. https://www.theatlantic.com/politics/archive/2014/05/moderates-who-are-they-and-what-do-they-want/370904/.

to protect the country's political future.[395] In contrast, moderates see many possible political futures. Political moderates maintain a mental flexibility for a vision of the future that is better but unknowable—a future with a familiar trajectory but also requiring ad-lib maneuvering in response to innumerable complex and unimaginable variables. Far-right conservative partisans have a vision of the future that is similar to the past, only better. How it gets better is left to the natural order of individual choice and the market, but closely held conservative values and principles remain the same. Any challenge to that vision is disruptive, and thus committed partisans keep their circle of friends limited to those who share the same political views, while moderates tend to have friends with differing political views.[396]

Moderates aren't predisposed to becoming partisans. Additional political knowledge and information doesn't often alter a moderate's path. The demand for political information, not the supply, is the main constraint on political knowledge. Thirty-five percent of moderates say they have tuned out politics, about the same percentage as liberals and conservatives.[397] But for those who remain tuned in, the selection of moderate political reporting and commentary has dwindled considerably. A generation ago when only a few network television channels vied for America's attention, political news needed to appeal to a broad range of political ideologies. A moderate presentation cut a path down the middle that touched different points of view without pandering to one particular political persuasion. A moderate presentation could increase the political knowledge of viewers with gentle persuasion. Cable news and the internet have reversed that trend. With so many more options

---

395    Hersch, *Politics Is for Power*, 104.

396    Will, *The Conservative Sensibility*, 195.

397    Ball, "Moderates: Who Are They?"

for political news, partisans can choose outlets that confirm their beliefs more than inform them.[398]

The challenge in bringing conservative America back to a more moderate position is that in this moment, political parties are weak, while partisanship is strong. The script has flipped. Gone is a party system that selected candidates who could appeal to a broad base of voters and charm the smoke-filled rooms of party bosses. It's replacement is a system that picks candidates that will be adored by base voters, the hard-cord partisans that volunteer and vote.[399]

That flip is not irreversible. American political winds have always shifted on the moderate to partisan curve over time. The Gilded Age from 1870 to 1900 was one of the most politically polarized eras in American history, as Southern Reconstruction divided Americans. Two generations and two world wars later, the country was in a more bipartisan mood, and moderates became favored by the electorate. A strong partisan era returned in the late 1960s with the Vietnam War, Malcolm X, Barry Goldwater, and Lyndon Johnson. That era gave way to a more moderate political climate in the 1970s and 1980s when the political distinctions between Republican and Democrat became less apparent. Partisanship trended once again in the 1990s, beginning with presidential candidate Pat Buchanan's "culture war"[400] and on through the Bush, Obama, and Trump presidencies. Historically, movements toward a more moderate political climate are often preceded by existential crises, such as war, while movements toward partisanship effort tend to follow times of relative comfort.

---

398    Will, *The Conservative Sensibility*, 96.

399    Klein, *Why We're Polarized*, 176.

400    Patrick Buchanan, *Address to Republican National Convention Speech*, Houston, Texas, August 17, 1992.

As the political winds change direction, so do political parties. Political parties aren't destined to last. The War of 1812 eliminated the Federalists.[401] Western expansion birthed the Democrats. The build up to the Civil War phased out the Whigs.[402] The trauma of the Great Depression caused Blacks to abandon the Republican Party, while business people did the opposite. The end of the Cold War and the beginning of the Digital Revolution has caused another reshuffling, with each political party pushing out to their partisan end—the Tea Party on the right, Black Lives Matter and #MeToo on the left. The partisan push has not been popular. In a recent Gallup poll, Americans' favorable opinion of the Republican Party declined to 37 percent, while 48 percent viewed the Democratic Party positively. The poll also showed 50 percent of U.S. adults identifying as political independents, presumably as a result of their rejection of the two major parties.[403]

Many would argue that a third political party is needed—one that fills the gap left by the respective parties moving to their extremes. In the same Gallup poll, a remarkable 62 percent of U.S. adults say the two parties do such a poor job representing the American people that a third party is needed.[404] It's a concept that's easy to want but difficult to have. America's "first past the post" electoral college forces a two-party system, which it has had since its founding. The presidential election winner needs the vote of at least 270 electors—one more than half of

---

401    https://en.wikipedia.org/wiki/Opposition_to_the_War_of_1812_in_the_United_States

402    Dave Roos, "Why the Whig Party Collapsed," History, January 8, 2021. https://www.history.com/news/whig-party-collapse.

403    Jeffrey M. Jones, "Support for Third U.S. Political Party at High Point," Gallup News, February 15, 2021. https://news.gallup.com/poll/329639/support-third-political-party-high-point.aspx.

404    Jones, "Support for Third U.S. Political Party."

all electors—to win the presidential election. As a result, third political parties struggle to mount a legitimate threat to the two major parties. The electoral college also acts as a governor on the partisan throttle. A major political party that becomes too partisan or too focused on single policies risks alienating moderate voters, being defeated in general elections, and losing electoral college votes. Some would argue the Republican Party is in such a position currently.

Barring a complete collapse of one or both political parties, the formation of a viable third political party with a moderate conservative platform is extremely unlikely. The political reawakening we need is a return to a more moderate Republican Party. A Republican Party with a thoughtful conservative agenda that preserves constitutional principles like liberty, free speech, freedom of religion, due process of law, and freedom of assembly without authoritarian, ultranationalist, and nativist ideologies and tendencies. To do so is a tall order.

We want change, but we tend to believe it's other people who need to do the changing. In the words of the great Russian author Leo Tolstoy, "Everyone thinks of changing the world, but no one thinks of changing himself."[405] We want others to see the world from our perspective, to believe the same things we do, to understand us. When that doesn't happen, we lash out, we get angry, we argue. But arguing inhibits our ability to understand how others see the world. Arguing with someone so they will change makes it less likely they will do so because no one changes until they feel understood.[406] There is no better place to see evidence of that truth than reading the comments following a political

---

405    Leo Tolstoy, quote, Books on the wall. https://booksonthewall.com/blog/leo-tolstoy-quote/.

406    Douglas Stone, Bruce Patton, Sheila Heen, and Roger Fisher, *Difficult Conversations: How to Discuss What Matters Most* (New York: Penguin Books, 1999), loc. 3312, Kindle.

post on social media. No one changes their mind on social media. Liberals don't become conservatives and conservatives don't become liberals by reading a *Facebook* post, watching a fifteen second *TikTok* video, or reading a 280-character tweet. Stories aren't posted to start a meaningful, thoughtful conversation that leads to greater understanding. Political posts on social media are used to bolster the identity of the person doing the posting, to rally similar-minded people, and to point out the differences between us and them. Such posts are more like small political conventions than an informed exchange between people with different beliefs.

If only we all shared the same beliefs. The model for change is easy when everyone believes the same things. It's easier to subject a group to power when there is uniformity. The more uneven the surface for the leader to look over, the more difficulty in getting the group to conform. Powerful people know this. This leads ambitious, less scrupulous leaders to try and control people by regulating what they know and, thus, what they think and say.[407] Ideally, leaders want to deliver a message to their followers that is simple and understandable, but not necessarily truthful.

Truth and power don't like to sit too close to one another. The acquisition of power by a leader eventually requires them to spread some fiction. But if a leader wants to spread the truth, eventually they will give up some power. People become united when they share and believe the same stories. Powerful leaders prefer injecting a bit of fiction into their stories because those stories become more compelling. Moreover, powerful leaders know that people want to feel the comfort of being united with those who are like-minded through the belief in a common story. Unity with others makes us feel powerful, while the truth is complex and divisive. When necessary, we selectively ignore the truth in order

---

407    Susskind, *Future Politics*, 128.

to keep our beliefs intact. Truth is optional. Power on the other hand is the foundation upon which we build our lives. Anytime we scheme, lie, negotiate, or try to prove something to ourselves or someone else, we are thinking in terms of power. The drive for power is about survival—emotional, psychological, spiritual, and physical survival. We believe that we must have power to overcome the people and problems that stand between our expectations and reality.[408] Power is the currency of control, and we want to control the world more than we want to understand it. Even when we do try to understand, it is usually in the hope of making the world around us easier to control.

Martin Luther King Jr. understood the difference between truth and power. He courageously spoke a truth that other powerful people already knew but preferred to keep concealed. The marches he led in Washington, D.C., Selma, and New York exposed truths about racism, poverty, and the Vietnam War that weren't understood by the entire nation. His message was disruptive but, at the same time, compelling. It fractured the narrative that the status quo was natural and acceptable. By speaking the truth, Dr. King conceded some of his power to political adversaries who didn't want that truth to be heard. It was a concession that cost him his own life but spurred a political movement that became part of his legacy.

Mark Twain once wrote that "A lie travels halfway around the world before truth puts its shoes on."[409] Lies about the risks we may face in the future prey on our fears of loss, suffering, or death. Those types of lies draw us together quickly, while truth takes time to digest, confirm,

---

408    Andrea Mathews, "Power Vs. Truth," *Psychology Today*, October 27, 2012. https://www.psychologytoday.com/us/blog/traversing-the-inner-terrain/201210/power-vs-truth.

409    Donald Rumsfeld, *Rumsfeld's Rules: Leadership Lessons in Business, Politics, War, and Life* (New York: Harper Collins, 2013), loc. 2121, Kindle.

and understand. Human beings are the most successful animals on the planet because of our ability to think and work together, not because of our individual rationality. Our strength lies in communicating simple messages quickly and effectively in wide-open forums, not pondering complexities in quiet solitude. As individuals, we know relatively little about the world and less with each passing day as history progresses and knowledge expands. Our ignorance remains unexposed and unexamined when we are locked inside like-minded groups and supplied with self-confirming news feeds. Most of our views are a result of groupthink that we hold on to out of loyalty, not individual rationalization. The scientific community trusts in the infallibility of facts and continues to believe it can win public debates by throwing the right facts around, despite empirical evidence to the contrary.[410] For example, as the COVID-19 pandemic wore on and scientific evidence became available on the efficacy of vaccination, scientists and physicians struggled to convince the majority of people in many states to get vaccinated.[411] When facts collide with beliefs, beliefs eventually win out, like water running over rock.

But a common set of beliefs is only valuable if the people sharing those beliefs can communicate with one another. While communicating with one another is easier than ever, that has not translated to political moderates becoming more active. College-educated voters, who lean more moderate to liberal,[412] are less active now than they were in the

---

410    Yuval Noah Harari, *21 Lessons for the 21st Century* (New York: Penguin Random House, 2018), p. 222.

411    Katie Adams, "States ranking by percentage of population vaccinated," Becker's Hospital Review website. https://tinyurl.com/5x5ew8rk. Accessed April 10, 2021.

412    "A Deep Dive Into Party Affiliation," Pew Research Center, April 7, 2015. https://www.pewresearch.org/politics/2015/04/07/a-deep-dive-into-party-affiliation/.

1960s. Back then, 10 percent to 17 percent of college-educated people were active on a campaign, and 11 percent to 24 percent attended a political rally. In 2012 and 2016, the numbers were one-third of that. Increasing the percentage of college-educated people may have made Americans more interested in politics, but it hasn't made us more politically active.[413]

Convincing the Republican Party to adhere to a more moderate agenda will require creating a vision that is more compelling to far-right conservatives than the current state of affairs. The far-right conservative agenda will not change in response to fighting but by building a model that makes the current partisan mindset obsolete. Battles waged against far-right conservatives are akin to making the same arguments for change against far-left liberals. It is an absolute waste of time. Trying to change people who don't think they have a problem is to spend time doing things that should never be done.

Creating a compelling model for a moderate conservative agenda requires action by people that are not prone to being politically active. To paraphrase author Stephen Covey, we cannot talk ourselves out of a problem that we behaved ourselves into.[414] The Republican Party has swung to the far right because of the persistent actions of those that wanted it to be that way. A swing back toward the middle will require similar actions by those that desire a more moderate agenda.

The swing toward the hard right was fueled by strong emotion—a response to Clinton, Obama, and Biden administrations with liberal agendas that threatened long-standing conservative positions. Passage of the Affordable Care Act, tax increases for high income earners,

---

413    Hersch, *Politics Is for Power*, 136.

414    Steven Covey, *The 7 Habits of Highly Effective People*, (New York: Rosetta Books, 1989), p. 186.

Dodd-Frank financial reform, and heavy handed regulatory measures by the Food and Drug Administration (FDA) and the Occupational Safety and Health Administration (OSHA) pushed Republicans to the right.[415] That move was accelerated by cultural events that moved Americans to the left, such as Black Lives Matter and the Occupy movements from 2014 to 2016, culminating in the election of Donald Trump in the fall of 2016.

A swing back toward a moderate agenda will require similar types of emotion but, in true moderate fashion, one that is different by degree, not principle. Anger is easy. Anyone can become angry. Becoming angry to the right degree, for the right purpose, in the right way, at the right time is difficult. To stand up for a moderate conservative approach is to stand against simplistic ideological debates. Life and politics are complex, and human beings are nuanced. Standing for mere platitudes and talking points reduces the rich, complicated, and complex life we have been given to something that is simple and easy but untrue.

For example, moderate conservatives are distrustful of a larger government providing more services. But that notion is too simplistic. We also want to live in a country that has a strong infrastructure with well-maintained roads, railways, rivers, and deep water ports. We want those who can't take care of themselves because of age, illness, or misfortune to be cared for with government assistance, but we also want those who can work to do so. We want our Second Amendment rights protected but would also like to see thorough background checks to prevent those who are mentally or behaviorally incapable of controlling their anger and impulses from owning a firearm. We want to pay as little as possible at the gas pump or to the utility companies and thus want to see coal,

---

415    Richard Williams, "How Obama Is Keeping Small Businesses Down," *US News*, March 25, 2014. https://tinyurl.com/d238yvh9.

oil, and natural gas continue to flow. At the same time, we realize that the future of energy from an environmental perspective has to put less carbon and other pollutants in the atmosphere. As such, we would like to see public investment in the development of those resources. We want to see as many children and adults as possible receive a quality education that provides them with opportunities in the digital economy. At the same time, all education should not be free. We value the things we pay for, and education should be something that each individual perceives as extremely valuable. We believe that legal immigration has been the backbone of American culture. At the same time, not every person in the world that wants to become an American can do so. The United States simply can't afford such a policy. We believe there are Americans that, by circumstances beyond their control—poverty, bad parenting, or bad luck—are forced into very difficult and destructive lives. Yet we also believe that some of those same people are a product of their own bad decisions.

Infrastructure, healthcare, energy, gun rights, education, and immigration are all horribly complex problems that do not have simplistic, ideologically consistent solutions. Rather, the possible solutions to complex problems are nuanced, iterative, and forever changing. Arriving at those types of solutions requires Americans to listen to ideas we don't agree with, remain skeptical of information that confirms our beliefs, empathize, see with new eyes, and reason for ourselves.

Swinging the conversations with fellow Republicans back to a more moderate agenda means engaging in difficult conversations with those who don't hold the same views. Many moderate conservatives fear those conversations because it forces them to state a position that makes them stand out from the Republican crowd. Most try to adopt a view that is so ambiguous that it will include everything and so popular that it will include everybody. But we are in a time when the world must be saved not through the complacent adjustment of the conforming majority but through the creative maladjustment of nonconformists. That requires one to open themselves up to criticism and ridicule. It is a path that can lead toward a harsh island of isolation and away from the security of like minds and nonjudgmental environments. To create such social change, you have to be a little crazy.[416]

More importantly, one has to act. As the old Chinese proverb says, the smallest actions are always better than the noblest intentions. Democracies do not reward intentions, nor do they elect those who keep their thoughts to themselves. Democracies reward groups that are engaged and share their thoughts with others. This has been the recipe for success for every revolution. To start a political movement, one doesn't need to know how many people agree. Instead, one needs to know how many supporters can effectively collaborate with others and network with them.[417]

But networking is not the same thing as leading and governing. Networks can overthrow but they don't govern. The gap between networking and leadership is where former President Obama fell. Obama was the chief accuser. He called out problems but offered no solutions. His modus operandi was to be aligned with the public's anger. A political movement that offers opposition without any propositions is like a dog that catches a car it's been chasing. The pursuit is only worthwhile if there is an end game to be played. Opposition without proposition was patently evident during the debate over building a wall on the U.S. southern border. Democratic opposition to a border wall was widespread, but the list

---

416    Nassir Ghaemi, *A First Rate Madness: Uncovering the Links* Between Leadership and Mental Illness (New York: Penguin Group, 2011), p. 114.

417    Yuval Noah Harari, *Homo Deus: A Brief History of Tomorrow* (New York: Penguin Random House, 2017), p. 132.

of viable alternatives to allowing illegal immigration to run unchecked was almost nil. Political movements, opposition, and accusations don't solve governance and policy problems, nor are elections the equivalent of governing.

With the country so evenly divided, the only path forward out of a political stalemate is for Republicans to come back to a more moderate agenda that appeals to moderate voters and brings electoral votes in the general election. The path there doesn't have to include an unconditional surrender to a liberal agenda. It should include a firm stand on the conservative principles in the Constitution that endure, accompanied by compromise on issues that will always change with time. The First and Second Amendments are not up for discussion. Replacing capitalism with communism is a hard stop. But federal income tax rates? Social program spending on education and healthcare? Regulation of large corporations? Aren't these issues open to negotiation? Couldn't reasonable people with different political ideologies disagree about the answers while still arriving at an agreeable compromise? To sit in a roomful of conservatives and beat up on liberal positions is easy. To work with liberals to create meaningful progress is difficult. The idealism born in the setting of like minds is quickly set aside when negotiation begins. As the Nobel Prize winning author John Galsworthy notes, "Idealism increases in direct proportion to one's distance from the problem."[418]

The basic political question of our day is whether the Constitution's primary purpose is the creation of a government architecture that ensures the protection of natural rights or whether its primary purpose is merely the creation of a government that facilitates effective majority rule. This is the perpetual back and forth of conservatives and progressives—the balance of the individual's right to freedom versus the majority's right

---

418    John Galsworthy, *Windows* (London, UK: Stage Door, 2017), p. 1.

to govern.[419] Government spending by a country cannot be too much or too little. Too much spending stifles corporate investment, while too little fails to provide the necessary roads, schools, and military that only a government is big enough to provide. Absent a strong system of taxation with too little spending, countries can end up with a government run by corrupt, poorly paid bureaucrats with a jerry-rigged infrastructure of utilities and roads that fail to serve the population.

The United States has always had a balance of conservatives and progressives. Pure capitalism without regulation is a figment of the conservative imagination. No nation, going back to the sixteenth century, has produced competitive industrial companies without significant help and protection from the state in the initial stages.[420] The same balance of conservatism and progressivism is necessary to work through social problems. To address poverty, liberals must realize that pouring more money into government programs is not a solution, while conservatives must realize that poverty is not a moral failure; racism, sexism and homophobia are real; and that incentives matter.[421]

For conservatives, there should be a difference between the nationalism of the partisan right and the patriotism that every American should feel. Patriots display pride in their people, a sense of shared identity and belonging. Such a feeling comes naturally for people born here but can be picked up by immigrants. Nationalists have similar feelings but couch their emotional identity in glorification. Their pride connects with prejudice. Patriots care about their members, but nationalists want to preserve what they see as a superior way of life. Nationalists are

---

419   Will, *The Conservative Sensibility*, 201.

420   Ruchir Sharma, *The Rise and Fall of Nations: Forces of Change in the Post-Crisis World* (New York: W. W. Norton, 2016), p. 141.

421   Tanner, *The Inclusive Economy*, 258.

suspicious of diversity. Patriots welcome it. Nationalists act in concert easily. Patriots are less restricted in what they perceive to be right, which makes their task of organizing effectively more onerous.[422]

Far-right conservatives value freedom. Far-left liberals value order. Moderates value both because freedom only matters once order has been established. Far-right conservatives see what is different about Americans. Far-left liberals stress what unifies mankind. Moderates stress that there will never be universal agreement on the best ways of living and social improvement, and we are best served by learning from one another.[423]

Knowledge itself is not power, but it is conducive to it.[424] The thinking that goes into gaining knowledge is difficult; that's why few people do it. It's easier to judge. We assume we know the truth, what is best—but what we need to explore are interpretations and judgments, not who is right and who is wrong.

History moves in leaps, not smoothly. The Soviet Union is a superpower until it's suddenly not. Mubarak was an immovable figure in Egypt, until he wasn't. Populism and polarization have taken over the American political conversation pushing moderates to the side – for now. Change only occurs when thoughtful people step forward. To create a leap, you have to do something. In the words of Nobel Peace Prize winner Mahatma Gandhi, "You may never know what results come from your actions. But if you do nothing, there will be no result."[425] One can avoid

---

422    Moffett, *The Human Swarm*, 369.

423    Kaplan, *The Revenge of Geography*, loc. 589.

424    Susskind, *Future Politics*, 1124.

425    Mahatma Gandhi, quote, Goodreads. https://www.goodreads.com/quotes/3343-you-may-never-know-what-results-come-of-your-actions.

the need to act, but no one can escape the consequences of failing to act. Karma has a way of finding those that wish to avoid responsibility. As the French poet Jean de La Fontaine once wrote, "A person often meets his destiny on the road he took to avoid it."

The United States has risen to its greatest achievements when Americans have felt the call to prove their mettle, morality, and the ability to win out over great odds. In this moment, we need thoughtful people to step forward, people who are brave enough to think for themselves, who can turn conversations that divide us into conversations that draw us together, who can transform their constructive words into meaningful actions, and who can inspire others to do the same. If not, populism, polarization, and hatred will continue to push our nation toward revolution and, like all great powers that have come before, the U.S. will collapse and be consigned to the study of historians. The question remains: will it be this generation that sees the great American experiment end, or will we deal with our problems in time to hand it off to another generation. It will be difficult, but as the great American broadcaster Edward Murrow once said, "Difficulty is the excuse history never accepts."[426] The choice is ours to make.

---

426    Edward R. Murrow, quote, Oracle website. https://scotgraden. com/2012/04/27/difficulty-is-not-an-excuse/.

# ACKNOWLEDGEMENTS

Books do not write themselves, and inspiration does not wash over authors just because we want it to. Eighteen months ago, my thoughts for this book were contained in several hundred pages of notes that I had jotted down from books, articles, talks, and conversations. I believed I had something important to say about what is happening in American culture, but untangling all those thoughts, ideas, beliefs, and assumptions and getting them on paper was a task I was incapable of on my own. What is contained in this book is the result of innumerable people who have thought long and hard about similar problems. If I have done my job, I have taken some of their thoughts and imprinted them with a new perspective that moves our national conversation forward. That job has not been a solo effort. I am deeply grateful to my wife, Meera, for her encouragement and support. Like no one else, she is able to hold up a mirror that allows me to see my ultimate blind spot: how I am perceived by others. Because she believes in the best of what I can be, her insight helps me become a better author and ultimately a better person.

I am indebted to my good friends (in alphabetical order), Ayesha Adams, Dan Bentzinger, Tre Brashear, Matt Callen, Mobi Khan, Ernie Moore, Dan Nuckolls, Tom Perry, Dan Pinheiro, Nancy Pinkston, Benjy Smith, Bailey Wall, and Jon Waltz who read early drafts of each chapter. If it's true that the measure of a friendship is the amount of time and energy people share, then I am lucky to count these people as true friends. Each of these people has been so kind to share his or her thoughts to help make this a better book and me a better author. Finally, a special thanks to my editors, Cathy Suter, Karin Rathert, Ashley Bunting, and Merack Publishing who helped take my erratic thoughts, too many anecdotes, and a mountain of data and turn them into a book. I am indebted to you for sharing your gifts with me with a patience and persuasiveness that allowed me to be heard.

# ABOUT THE AUTHOR

Alan Scarrow, MD, JD is a neurosurgeon in Springfield, Missouri.

Dr. Scarrow has practiced neurosurgery for 18 years and has served in numerous leadership roles, including President of the Mercy Health System in Springfield and President of the Congress of Neurological Surgeons. He has given over 50 lectures around the world and has authored numerous peer-reviewed and invited articles.

Dr. Scarrow received his medical education from Case Western Reserve University School of Medicine, Cleveland, Ohio. He also holds a Doctor of Jurisprudence (JD) from Case Western Reserve University School of Law and a Bachelor of Science Degree in Electrical Engineering from the University of Nebraska.

He completed his Neurosurgery Residency at the University of Pittsburgh after doing a Surgical Internship at University Hospitals of Cleveland. In addition, he completed a one-year Congress of Neurological Surgeons Public Policy Fellowship in Washington, D.C.

He is a native of Fairbury, Nebraska, and is married to Meera Scarrow, MD, JD. who is an OB/GYN at Mercy Health System in Springfield. They have three children. In their off time, the Scarrows enjoy working on their cattle farm.

Made in the USA
Las Vegas, NV
01 January 2024

83779731R00132